Dr Pierre Dukan
The Dukan Diet

Desserts and Patisseries

with Rachel Levy's
invaluable contribution

DER &
JHTON

First published in France in 2011 by J'ai lu

First published in Great Britain in 2013 by Hodder & Stoughton
An Hachette UK company

1

Copyright © 2013 Dr Pierre Dukan

Photos © Natacha Nikouline
© Éditions J'ai lu, 2011
Collection managed by Ahmed Djouder

A CIP catalogue record for this title is available from the British Library

Trade paperback ISBN 978 1 444 75795 8
Ebook ISBN 978 1 444 75796 5

Translated by Morag Jordan
Designed by non-ninon.com | angledrotsg.com
Typeset in Century Gothic by Bobby&Co
Printed and bound in China by C&C Offset Printing Company, Ltd

Hodder & Stoughton policy is to use papers that are natural, renewable and
recyclable products and made from wood grown in sustainable forests.
The logging and manufacturing processes are expected to conform to the
environmental regulations of the country of origin.

Hodder & Stoughton Ltd
338 Euston Road
London NW1 3BH

www.hodder.co.uk

Contents

Writing this book, I have kept to one of the promises I made myself, which was never to offer my readers, who had placed their affectionate trust in me, anything pointless or unnecessary, anything that had no proven, legitimate purpose.

If you have bought *The Dukan Diet Desserts and Patisseries*, the likelihood is that you have already read my other books. As with a meal, you don't get into my method by starting at the end, with the puddings; you work your way through the menu, following the diet's main road map as it unfolds with its 100 foods and four phases.

You are familiar with my method, you have probably tried it, and, if you are still reading what I write, this is because you have appreciated my help. You are part of a following I don't know personally but for whom – and I will say this as plainly as possible – I feel great affection. Why? Quite simply because my life has changed since you started to exist for me.

I have always been a happy man. However, for the past couple of years this simple happiness has bordered on blissful joy. At almost every moment in my day, I think about you. First during my consultations when I see my patients, but also when I receive the piles of letters sent by my readers, emails from internet users, all the messages, questions and calls for help from the people who have subscribed to my online coaching and to whom I reply both personally and through live chat sessions.

At my age, neither money nor fame can give me what I get from having you by my side. There, I have said it, I am talking to friends; there is more enjoyment and more warmth and it frees up the imagination...

There will be those who are thinking that I've already written many books, which is certainly true, but not a single one is surplus to requirements. Each book has its own proper place and plays an essential part in helping people follow my diet.

I realize, though, that writing an entire book about puddings might seem counterintuitive for someone who has spent most of their working life helping people to fight weight problems.

Where did the idea for this book come from?

I was far younger and more fervent when I laid down the foundations for my method, and my diet, which turned into an eating programme, was limited to basic foods, the 72 high-protein low-fat foods and then the 28 vegetables. Back in those days, research was still going on into low-fat dairy products; sweeteners were not used to anything like their full potential; low-fat sliced meats were not available, nor were seafood sticks; and, as yet, I had no idea that oat bran even existed.

Nowadays, circumstances have improved radically. New foods and new ways of adding taste, new cooking utensils and new manufacturing methods are being developed all the time, which means my proteins and vegetables come more attractively presented and with improved performance.

As the years go by, more and more people, especially women, are using my method and this means more and more people in many countries who love eating. When millions of women are searching for some way of creating great music from very simple notes, something flavoursome and sophisticated using the basics, they end up performing a miracle. This is how *The Dukan Diet Desserts and Patisseries* came about.

It all happened with those ingredients that are most vital for success – time, numbers and motivation. Millions of women who love the taste of sugar; years of individual research and exchanging ideas; and a powerful motivation to lose weight without any sadism or masochism have gradually produced this composition of dessert and patisserie recipes, which I have orchestrated and conducted so that my 'sugarholics' would not despair.

I must confess that I feel a particular fondness and compassion for these women, and the men too, because as a child I also had a sweet tooth; and I live with a woman and two children who love sweet things, which says it all.

Already for some years I had been able to tell my patients and readers that they could indeed lose weight while limiting their frustration. Today, I can assure them that they can shed their pounds without regaining them while at the same time giving themselves some pleasure. Better still, I would say that knowing how to produce desserts and patisserie from the foods in my diet means they have less frustration to cope with, so they will lose weight more easily. They will then stand a far better chance of stabilizing their weight over the long term.

I have already had many opportunities to voice my opinion that pleasure and displeasure are what underlie the problem of putting on weight and losing weight. Apart from incidental, accidental or genetic reasons, people put on weight to compensate for experiencing suffering or distress or displeasure, and we can only lose weight by lessening the frustration involved with dieting and by rediscovering pleasure.

If many diets and methods fail, it is because they do not take into account this idea of pleasure/displeasure which lies at the very heart of any motivation we feel and which over time sustains our commitment. I am fortunate to have extensive experience of working in this field, enough to have freed myself from the pseudo-facts that come from the world of academic nutrition. According to this young branch of scientific study, which is attempting to match up to the hard sciences – those of figures and equations – people put on weight whenever the body's calorie intake is greater than the calories recorded and used by this same body. So get your calculators out and forget everything else.

This sort of system might work for a machine, a prisoner in a cell, an infant in its cradle or a laboratory rat in a cage, since they have no other choice but to eat what others decide to give them. However, for you, dear readers, things are quite different, as you walk around with a cheque book or credit card and are free to buy whatever you fancy; you can purchase whatever foods you choose and know your store cupboards are full of them.

How do people come to put on weight?

Stop and think for a moment, and ask yourself what was it that made you eat those foods that resulted in you putting on the weight, pound after pound, that you hate so much.

From what I have understood and heard from the vast majority of people who have confided in me every day over such a long time now, this is what sticks in my mind.

When you eat more than your biological requirements so that you end up putting on weight, you are not doing this to satisfy a genuine hunger because the billions of cells in your body are not getting enough glucose. Even less is it about you consuming the 'normal' quantity of calories and nutrients defined by nutritional science as necessary.

It is about something else altogether. You are using these foods to provide a most valuable commodity in our fabulously rich but equally tough world – they produce certain types of sensation which, on reaching the brain, are able to create pleasure. And they can do something even more sophisticated – they can neutralize displeasure. Let me explain.

Let's imagine that your family life, love life or career are not providing you with enough pleasure and that this is preventing you from achieving fulfilment, a little like a plant that is not getting sufficient sun or water. There is a strong likelihood that you will feel tempted to eat a food that will make its way through your body, triggering pleasure inside you. You don't take this decision to eat consciously or deliberately; it is made way down in your old brain, in your animal brain, which controls your survival. There are two tiny centres based in the hypothalamus and the limbic system which control attachment, as well as sexuality, territory and so on.

Now let's imagine that it is not a lack of pleasure that is the problem but rather an excess of displeasure, as you are assailed by too much aggravation and stress. The same centres in your brain start to react instinctively and automatically. You treat yourself to some food to neutralize the displeasure and prevent the unalleviated suffering from accumulating and leading you step by step towards depression. Once again it is not your conscious and wilful self making the decision here but your in-built survival programme which you share with all mammals. In this case, the process is slightly more complex and indirect; your brain does not produce pleasure to add to your fulfilment but to neutralize the excess of displeasure you are experiencing. This may all seem very complicated but it couldn't be simpler. The way that man and higher animals work emotionally and instinctively is governed by a two-sided rudder; one side heads towards pleasure, the other towards displeasure. There is, however, only one intangible instruction, which is to navigate by bringing the helm back to the middle. If the winds in your life steer your navigation towards lack of pleasure or far too much displeasure, your survival mechanisms swing into action and steer you in the right direction to get you back on course.

You will have realized that people put on weight by eating more energy than their bodies require because they want to find some pleasure. So how can we give up using food as a crutch and pit ourselves against such ingrained survival behaviour in order to lose our surplus pounds?

Obviously, declaring that our calorie intake has to be reduced will not suffice. We will need to find a way of producing pleasure other than by eating food that is too rich and therefore bad for us.

Producing pleasure while at the same time attempting to lose weight

For someone attempting to lose weight the very best pleasure of all is precisely that – losing weight and losing it quickly, especially at the outset, so that you really believe you're going to slim down. This generates success which in turn generates pleasure. And for this to happen you need a diet that gets off to a cracking start, which is why my first phase is called the 'Attack' – it lasts only a few days but it will upset your scales.

For a woman especially, another pleasure is to see and feel her body change as she touches it or finds she can now easily slip into clothes that have long been unworn, and she is quite happy to look at herself whenever she passes in front of a mirror.

Creating success is yet another source of pleasure and with it come self-confidence and self-esteem – definitely something that will get your brain to agree to cut down on pleasure derived from food.

There is also the surprising and unfortunately underrated pleasure that we get simply from being physically active. In the field of neurosciences, there have been recent discoveries not widely known among the medical profession and of which the general public is quite unaware. It has been found that for the average individual, a tolerable level of physical activity three hours per week makes the muscles and brain produce three neurotransmitters: serotonin, which gives us joy and pleasure in being alive; dopamine, which gives us energy and the desire to be alive; and norepinephrine, which stimulates and maintains our alertness, attentiveness and level of consciousness.

To sum up, physical activity, and walking in particular, is absolutely vital in my method: 20 minutes a day in the Attack phase; 30 minutes in Cruise; 25 in Consolidation; and 20 minutes a day for the rest of your life in permanent Stabilization.

At the same time and in order to neutralize displeasure, I have always allowed you the 100 EAT AS MUCH AS YOU WANT FOODS so that you can avoid the frustration and suffering that come from feeling constantly hungry.

Monitoring and support also anaesthetize frustration, which is why I have set up an online coaching service that offers a personal relationship and, most important, a daily to-and-fro dialogue.

Trying to lose weight with others in a forum, or by contributing to a blog, creates a feeling of togetherness as you follow in the footsteps of others, and this also reduces the displeasure and frustration that often accompany dieting.

It is possible to produce pleasure with the 100 foods!

Finally, and this is the point I wanted to make, it is indeed possible to create pleasure through eating but without allowing yourself to get carried away by the easily and immediately available high-sugar, high-fat and high-calorie foods that people usually succumb to. With some thought, and by focusing on being inventive, you can prepare meals that give you pleasure while at the same time sticking to the 100 allowed foods and extra tolerated foods in my method.

There were already 1,200 recipes available on the www. regimedukan.com website. Thanks to the research and resourcefulness of all the members of the Dukan Diet community, it is now possible to produce a whole book devoted to the culmination of pleasure when eating and sharing mealtimes: DESSERTS AND PATISSERIES! That is what this book is all about and it marks one more step towards overcoming weight problems. It provides the answer to what I see as the main, but hidden, reason why people become overweight, which is that they use rich, sweet and fatty foods, foods that appeal enormously to our senses, to create pleasure or neutralize displeasure. Here we are at the heart of the matter, so let's see now what you can get from a book devoted entirely to desserts and patisseries that will 'help you slim'.

The brain and pleasure

Knowing how to whip up an oat bran galette in a few minutes, or how to produce a batch of muffins, a cheesecake, a gingerbread loaf, a custard flan or mousse in just as little time – and having absorbed and internalized all this knowledge while at the same time losing weight quickly and permanently – will make what you've learnt part of your survival behaviour patterns, in other words patterns that are 'highly rewarding and will be remembered forever'. Developed during times of hardship and restriction, this expertise becomes a luxury and guarantees security in the Stabilization period. How could you possibly stop using tools and behaviour patterns as useful and effective as these?

Before giving you these recipes with instructions about how to use them, I would like to take a closer look at what I have just told you about pleasure. You may well think that I'm putting too much emphasis on these complex neuroscience ideas. However, apart from their being a subject I find really exciting, I think that if you take heed of them you can really find a lot to help you here, which is why I want to come back to those ideas and describe them in greater detail.

I believe that nowadays we live in a disillusioned world, a world bereft of ideals where our lives are governed by the economic model, the material world and consumption, without any fervour, any dreams or any magic.

I sincerely believe that in each human being is a curious mind that strives to feed on information and achieve greater things by leaving our humdrum reality behind in a bid to reach for something higher. But our society's economic model, with its emphasis on consumption and suppression, drags the curious mind back down to the bottom. And at this bottom is 'food', food that makes us fat.

I tell you without any exaggeration or pomposity that what I am trying to outline to you, to my mind, can and must become the next ideal for man – and this is to understand how our brains are programmed, so that this understanding helps us enjoy being alive and want and need to be alive. And I think that the first people who can benefit from this, and benefit the most, are those who are overweight, obese and depressed.

Comprehending how the most complex instrument or object in the known world works is so incredibly beautiful and, above all, so useful in a practical sense that it will satisfy our insatiable need to understand and explore. What is more, it will give us, and you who are reading my book, the surest means of steering yourself towards the purpose of all life – which is to exist while at the same time taking pleasure from existing and snatching happiness from life.

This questioning has grown out of my 40 years of work battling weight problems and is a part of it. My experience, gained from meeting so many patients desperate to lose weight, has convinced me that weight problems always develop when there is a background of dissatisfaction, anxiety, suffering, vulnerability and intolerance of stress. I concluded, therefore, that being overweight was the sociological marker for an unsatisfactory lifestyle, due either to some temporary or longstanding difficulty in finding self-fulfilment or to the accumulation of stress.

The vast majority of people who come to my consultations to get help and lose weight abhor being overweight. They are willing to make huge efforts to lose (or lose again) their surplus pounds, but acknowledge that they gained them totally against their will so as to soothe some other suffering even greater than that of being overweight.

Always remember that YOU, the entity that makes you who you are, consists of a body and a mind. Your body is controlled quite automatically; this is done through reflexes and is based on a simple law: the law of returning to and maintaining balance which has been given the awful name 'homeostasis' by scientists. It explains physiology and survival for all higher creatures, man included. This vital principle allows the body to set in motion the right measures so that it returns to a state of balance whenever it strays away from it. So when the body is attacked externally, it reacts by adapting its internal environment. Whenever you don't have enough water and start to become dehydrated your brain triggers thirst, which will make you drink. Or again, whenever you find yourself in a cold environment, your body will shiver to produce heat and warm you up. Thousands of such examples show how your life is being constantly protected.

Having observed the signs throughout my long career, and from questioning my patients, I have been able to record and establish that in just the same way as there is homeostasis to control our vital functions, there is a homeostasis that controls our access to pleasure. What is interesting about this discovery is that here again everything works automatically and subconsciously.

So whenever there happens to be a chronic lack of pleasure in your life or if you are overwhelmed by too much stress, which amounts to the same thing, your brain is programmed to make you find sufficient pleasure again and by all available means, so that you don't give up on what is your life's central project – which is to stay alive. When my patients are unable to get enough satisfaction and fulfilment from their daily life, I witness time and again how their behaviour patterns instinctively take hold so that they reap some satisfaction and fulfilment at whatever cost and wherever possible. The purpose behind this instinctive reaction is to prevent the levels of pleasure from dropping below a threshold – which I call the minimum pleasure threshold – beyond which our desire to be alive fades until we sink into depression and then extinction mode.

The law of pleasure

Why, and based on which law or reason, do we need pleasure to survive?

Because – and all mammals function this way – in the very depths of our animal brain we have a centre that automatically and subconsciously controls our existence, so that our main objective is to remain alive and so that we make every effort to live and not die.

I call this centre our 'pulsar', because it automatically sends out a life beat similar to that from a foetus' heart, which appears as soon as the ovum – the meeting, then the fusion, of the oocyte and the sperm – has developed sufficiently to be no longer simply a part of the mother. This pulsation starts very early on, during the first months in the womb, and stops only with death. The intensity of the beat varies according to life's ups and downs and, critically, can drop during major depression, which can lead to the pulse stopping and to suicide.

For a long time, the question that played on my mind, and which I finally managed to answer, was what was the force or energy driving the pulsar, 'feeding' it and keeping it beating to ensure our survival? We are now reaching the area right at the nub of the matter; here is where we get to understand the most basic fundamentals of life.

To understand how our pulsar works, we have to see it as an engine that produces the most precious thing in the world – irrepressible energy and the desire to be alive. The engine driving us is steered by a rudder that guides and directs this tumultuous, chaotic force. The tiller for this rudder is the two small centres I have already told you about: the centre for pleasure and the one for displeasure, controlling reward and punishment.

Our instinctive behaviour patterns, which include those that compel us to feed ourselves and reproduce, are genetically programmed to steer us towards pleasure and away from displeasure. Much of life's mystery and interest lies in getting these behaviour patterns to be successful and effective. And, without us even being aware of it, what life is seeking, what the pulsar's energy, the rudder's directions and our search behaviour patterns aim to find, through us and by any means possible, is precisely pleasure and always, always pleasure.

The question that you rightly ought to ask yourself is: why is pleasure so crucial? We could live quite well without pleasure, couldn't we? Here we are right at the very crux of existence and, once the demonstration is over, if you have really understood it and if you start to put this knowledge to good use, you will possess all you need to make your life a happy one.

Before going any further, let's go back to the word 'pleasure', which must have been one of the first that man invented. Nowadays, as a word so commonly used, its meaning has become vague. When we talk about pleasure, we tend to think only of the simple, pleasant feeling that 'gives us pleasure'. This is correct up to a point, but what is crucial is that we think that this feeling, other than the pleasure experienced, is at the same time 'doing us some good'.

You may well think that this is just a nuance of no great significance. Well, think again! There's a world of difference between pleasure and doing us good, and you need to understand this world of difference. But don't worry, it's really simple – just like life.

Concealed by the feeling of 'enjoyable pleasure' that we all know so well, an inconspicuous passenger is in fact travelling alongside, the very essence of what we are all, without knowing it, searching for from the first to the last day of our lives: vital energy, the life force that drives us to stay alive and not die. Making the journey together, pleasure is the first to make its presence felt as it provides us with an enjoyable feeling before it fades away. The second passenger, invisible and left alone on the track, carries on with its journey which takes it to the pulsar. This passenger's mission is in fact to transfer the energy it is carrying to the pulsar, to recharge it and in so doing keep the cycle of life going: a pulsar that pulsates, a rudder that steers, instinctive behaviour patterns that gather pleasure and the accompanying nourishment that will come and recharge the pulsar.

Through this mechanism, you need to understand that if you don't harvest enough of pleasure's twin nourishments, and do this over the long term, the strength of your pulsar is likely to weaken and with it your vital energy, quite simply your desire to live.

This vital nourishment, as it travels along discreetly, concealed by pleasure's exuberance, is so obviously and intuitively part and parcel of life that it has never been given a name. Since it gets assimilated either with pleasure or with the vague concept of our instinct for self-preservation, it has been overlooked. In order to secure its existence, define its territory, pinpoint it and be able to use it, I had to give it a name. So I called it 'bene-satisfaction', to combine both satisfaction and benefit in a single word. I am not trying to give you a lesson in physiology or philosophy; I am taking you very concretely to the subject that interests us both, namely your weight problems.

To understand how in practice not getting enough bene-satisfaction can affect the quality of your experience of life, let's take the example of depression, which is unfortunately all too common nowadays.

If you are emotionally vulnerable and suffer a string of stressful and upsetting events, the amount of pleasure you get out of life is going to run dry. The bene-satisfaction you produce will drop too, your life pulsar will no longer get recharged and the vital energy that it gives out will dwindle. Your mood will darken, plans will fall apart, your vital energy will plummet, fatigue will plague you the whole time and sleep will be hard to find. One morning the urge to get out of bed will be gone and no pleasure will be got from life. Everything will stop.

In times gone by, having depression could mean ending up in a mental home. These days, anti-depressants take over the role that bene-satisfaction no longer performs, which is to secrete the chemical neurotransmitters than can recharge life's pulsar.

Being overweight and controlling pleasure

Now we are coming to the area that interests us – being overweight and how this is directly linked with controlling pleasure.

You get far less bene-satisfaction when you are living through periods of dissatisfaction and stress, dreary, gloomy times when you have trouble finding any fulfilment. Your whole body suffers because of this and it goes into a state of alert that triggers behaviour patterns designed to snatch some pleasure in any shape or form.

People who have a tendency to find comfort in food will also seek pleasure from eating the most indulgent foods available, those with the most taste, the most fats, the most sugar and calories. They will put on weight. Others will turn towards different sources of pleasure unconnected with food. Nourishment that does not come from food may be emotional, physical, aesthetic or spiritual, but all these sources of pleasure, though appearing in very different guises, produce, convey and share the same precious bene-satisfaction without which our pulsar, and life itself, will fade away. So what are these other sources of non-food nourishment and the behaviour patterns designed to harvest this nourishment and satisfy our human needs, the higher needs of our species?

I've spent the past 20 years identifying these great natural needs of man, needs which when satisfied help maintain our capacity for life. Despite being universal and giving structure to the human psyche, these needs do not easily find ways to express themselves in modern cultures that tend to neglect them. It was primitive man, naked and unpolluted by his culture, who shed light on this research. You will readily recognize sexuality and more broadly love, couples, caring for children, being parents and so on. If approached in the right way, pleasure can spring from these needs. Just think about all the suffering caused when these people and things are absent from our lives. You will identify universal behaviour patterns linked to society and finding one's proper place within the group, whether it be using charisma to lead or employing the skills and gifts you were born with. Whereas dominance and natural aptitudes were relevant and effective in primitive cultures, where there was the need to hunt and gather and for manual prowess and aggressiveness to protect the group, nowadays in the narrow professional work arena such needs are discredited.

It is with immense pleasure that I've tracked down these natural needs of man. I have managed to identify 10 of them and, despite exhaustive efforts, I have been unable to find an 11th. I have grouped them together, calling them my '10 Pillars of Happiness', and my next book will be about them.

Among them you will recognize an enormous need that you know well, the need to eat and to feed yourself to stay alive, of course; but, perhaps even more important, to produce the feeling of pleasure under whose cover bene-satisfaction, its companion and counterpart, travels too.

It is becoming increasingly difficult to satisfy most of these great natural needs in our contemporary societies. The trouble with these needs is that they are free and so they compete with the artificial needs dreamed up for our consumer society. Once the great avenues leading to natural pleasure and happiness are closed and the need for bene-satisfaction comes to claim its due, your survival behaviour patterns drive you towards the simple and immediate pleasure you can find in food. This is how most weight gain starts and then develops.

Always keep in mind that the whole complex machinery ensuring our survival was established in our genes when our species – *Homo sapiens* – was born. At that time the environment was totally different, so the first commandment for survival in such huge, cold and hostile spaces was to find enough food and energy simply to stay alive. If you spend some time thinking about it, you'll see that most of the food you find 'good' is almost always the food with the most calories. The richer a food is, the more fat it contains; especially if it is sweet, we crave it all the more, wanting it so much that our resistance is broken.

We should also realize that since the first man appeared this initial programming has not changed one iota. Children born today in Paris or New York 'leave the production line' with exactly the same engine as did Cro-Magnon infants. Over the millennia, environment, cultures, traditions, religions and economic imperatives have all desperately tried to temper our biological instincts, but to no avail. Our need for sensations from food, tied up with needing high-calorie foods, stands there like a permanent totem pole, and towering over all these sensations sugar exerts its magic.

Scientific studies show that our genes developed in times of shortage when the only sugar available was to be found in the berries or wild fruit that the birds were gracious enough to leave for us. Anthropologists estimate that, in those far-off times, our sugar consumption must have been 2kg (4½lb) per person per year. In 1830, we had reached 5kg (11lb) per year. By 2000, this had increased to an incredible 35kg (5½ stone) a year in France, and to 70kg (11 stone) in the United States. These few figures say it all.

Recipes for pleasure...but without the calories

Luckily for us, even if it is impossible to alter our genes and our instincts, today there are new ways of skirting round this danger, by using recent tools that are not yet perfect but are being constantly improved through research. These tools are decoys; they are products that manage to dissociate what nature has associated in us, pleasure and calories. You are familiar with sweeteners; they give us the taste of sugar but without the calories. Personally, I feel that as we battle with weight problems, these decoys offer us a huge advance. There are many different food decoys now, a large number of 'reduced' fat and salt products.

However, the second-generation decoys, the substances I have most worked on and the ones I believe to have the most to offer and the brightest future, are food flavourings. As yet they are not well known among the wider public and I would like to see this change. A food flavouring is a taste and a smell that carries the essence of a food and its neurological signature. A drop of vanilla flavouring in an egg custard is enough to transform it into something magical, so that our brains enjoy quite a different experience. Add a drop of rum flavouring to fruit juice and we start dreaming of tropical climes; a drop of Roquefort flavouring can elevate a boring yoghurt dressing on to a different level. The leanest of beef burgers taste of fat and grease when a drop of melted butter flavouring is added. Look out for these flavourings – they have not yet given up all their secrets, nor have all their riches been exhausted.

Today, with this little book of a hundred or so recipes, made in part with these decoys, I am offering you an arsenal that is meant to create some pleasure when instead you expect restriction and frustration. The words 'patisserie' and 'desserts' seldom get a mention once you embark on serious dieting and really want to lose weight.

I am taking this risk because all the people who have tried these recipes have got further with their dieting and stuck with it longer, which is a good sign. I sincerely hope that these recipes – and I've tasted most of them! – will help you.

All the dessert recipes in this book are allowed in my diet. Nevertheless, you must remember that certain recipes use wheat bran, cornflour and fat-reduced cocoa powder. These foods do not come with the words AS MUCH AS YOU WANT, unlike the 100 foods in the two actual weight-loss phases of my diet. The bran is limited and the tolerated foods are just that – tolerated foods whose use is restricted both with regard to quantity and how many can be used together. Always remember to check the list of these foods and how to use them (see page 23).

Another important point is that there are only six recipes that include fruit. Fruit first appears in phase 3 of my diet, Consolidation, as you will see from the recipe selection.

Another important subject is sweeteners and here my position is clear – I advocate using them without the slightest hesitation. The argument that using sweeteners only encourages a sweet tooth does not stand up to scrutiny. In all my long years as a nutritionist, I have never come across a patient, and especially not a female patient, who had lost their craving for sugar after following a diet without sugar or sweeteners. There is no point in creating unnecessary frustration. You will come across different sweeteners in these recipes, in part to ring the changes but also because the most suitable sweetener has been selected for the recipe, so that it fits with the taste of the dish or how it is cooked.

Finally, it would be very cowardly indeed to finish this introduction without mentioning chocolate. For any nutritionist working with people to help them fight their weight problems, chocolate causes the greatest mischief. A large number of people who are prone to gaining weight turn out to be utterly defenceless when faced with this temptation. If this is true of you, there is only one solution – COCOA. Cocoa is the specific active ingredient in chocolate; the rest is just white sugar and cocoa fat. If you use fat-reduced cocoa powder, you are allowed cocoa in controlled quantities. It takes only a single teaspoonful of cocoa powder, as long as it is pure and fat-reduced, and you can enjoy all the flavour of chocolate.

Knowing how to focus on yourself

At this point, if you've followed me in my thesis about the need for pleasure, fulfilment and happiness and understood what I have said, this book will bring you a gift that you were unaware of before you started reading it – namely, bene-satisfaction and the vital energy we need to be successful in an undertaking as difficult and unnatural as trying to lose weight.

Since we are talking about 'nature' in general and ours – our human nature – in particular, you will be well aware that we live in a world based on an economic model where 70% of our food is now industrially manufactured. Whatever age you are, you must be very used to eating factory-baked cakes and puddings with artificial icing, food colouring, additives, creamy fillings and transfats. What I am giving you here in this book are desserts and cakes that you can make yourself using natural products. I am aware that making time for yourself doesn't quite fit with the spirit of our modern times, but if you are trying to lose weight, to some extent you will have realized that the spirit of our times has led to many things, including your extra pounds, and that by actually cooking for yourself you are focusing on yourself too. And if you have children, they'll be surprised, and pleasantly so, as I promise you that your cooking and baking will be a way for you to show them that there are lovely sweet things to eat other than industrially manufactured biscuits and artificial confectionery.

As I wrap up this introduction, it occurs to me that, given that this is a book about desserts and patisseries, I may have worn out some of my readers by examining in detail a topic so dear to me – the search for happiness and deciphering our ultimate reasons for being alive. I did this because I wanted to focus on the aspiration in each of us to strive for higher things and, if you found it hard going, don't worry, as we're now going to turn our attention to the concrete and to the sensual appeal of the recipes. I am sure that the seeds sown today will go on to take root and grow in your mind as there is nothing more fundamental than knowing how we humans work. Your weight and how it gets out of balance are very much part and parcel of this realm of knowledge.

KEY INGREDIENTS FOR DUKAN DESSERTS AND PATISSERIES AND WHERE TO FIND THEM

Oat bran

Oat bran is one of the ingredients on which my diet and my method are based, which of course holds true for *The Dukan Diet Desserts and Patisseries* too. In addition to its medicinal action, as far as I know oat bran is the only foodstuff that can claim to induce weight loss. Capable of absorbing 30 times its volume in water, it swells up in the stomach and makes you feel full very quickly. Oat bran sticks to the food in the intestines and is taken away with it in the stools.

However, do be careful which oat bran you buy as the different sorts available are not all of equal merit. For oat bran to be medicinal and not just for cooking purposes, it has to be produced by grinding and separating the grain from the bran in a very particular way, i.e. with specific milling and sifting. Working with Finnish agricultural engineers, I determined that this was M2bis milling and B6 sifting.

Ordinary oat bran is available in all health-food shops but medicinal oat bran can be found only in some pharmacies and health-food stores or on the internet at www.mydukandietshop.co.uk.

Wheat bran

There are few other foods that contain as much insoluble fibre as wheat bran and it is widely used to prevent constipation. Its texture and hardness can give some recipes density and consistency. It is available in health-food stores, in some pharmacies and on the internet at www.mydukandietshop.co.uk.

Sweeteners

All the sweeteners that you are able to buy nowadays can be used for cooking. They have all been subjected to extensive scientific research to ensure that they are completely safe for us to eat.

You will come across a certain number of sweeteners in this book which I have selected because they taste best for the recipe or because they withstand cooking: Canderel and Canderel vanilla sticks (aspartame); crystallized stevia (stevia), for all cold desserts or those that are slightly warmed, and for any intense cooking; liquid Hermesetas (cyclamate and saccharin); and Splenda (sucralose). Canderel, Splenda and liquid Hermesetas are available in supermarkets; and crystallized stevia can be found in pharmacies, health-food stores, supermarkets and on the internet at www.mydukandietshop.co.uk.

Cornflour

Cornflour is corn starch and is not a food that you are allowed to have 'as much as you want' of. It is a tolerated food rationed to 1 tablespoonful per day. I have given cornflour this 'tolerated' status as it is extremely useful for binding sauces and making desserts and light cakes. Cornflour does not contain any gluten.

Fat-reduced cocoa powder

Fat-reduced cocoa is the active ingredient in chocolate; the rest is just fat and sugar. This cocoa allows you to produce wonderful, light desserts and patisseries without depriving yourself of the taste of chocolate. However, do be careful– plain cocoa and sugar-free cocoas, such as the fabulous Van Houten, do not fit the bill. What you need is sugar-free, fat-reduced cocoa and again this is a tolerated food.

This type of cocoa is not yet sold in supermarkets but you can find it on the internet at www.mydukandietshop.co.uk. and it is also available in certain pharmacies and health-food stores.

Food flavourings

As with cocoa, I have already mentioned food flavourings, which are an extraordinary concept with a great future ahead of them in the fight against weight problems. I have done a lot of work on the physiology of this phenomenon which enables us to use an array of powerful, original smells and flavours without the calories that usually come with them. Food flavourings throw the way wide open for my diet by making it possible to combine unlimited quantities with unlimited flavours. Unfortunately these flavourings are not widely available and for the time being can be found only on the internet at www.mydukandietshop.co.uk.

Agar-agar and gelatine

Up until now we have been mostly familiar with gelatine, a protein product that usually comes in leaf form or as powder.

Mainly of animal origin (bovine or porcine), the leaves need to be rehydrated in cold water before use. When the leaves have softened, they must be wrung out, then added to hot but not boiling liquid to dissolve, then the liquid is left to cool down and turn to gel. Gelatine is bought primarily from supermarkets. (To eat Kosher or Halal, you can also find special varieties of gelatine made from fish by-products – buy these from Kosher or Halal shops.)

However, it is just as easy to use agar-agar, a noble gelling agent from the seas, extracted from seaweed that is collected far from the shores. To make custards, jellies, etc., you simply mix a 2g sachet of agar-agar powder into 500ml (18fl oz) of any liquid – milk, flavoured tea, herb tea, soya juice, fruit juice, meat or vegetable stock – and heat the mixture until it boils and then leave it to cool. The less liquid you use, the firmer the texture of the dish will be. Agar-agar is available on the internet at www.mydukandietshop.co.uk. or in health-food and Asian food stores.

When should you eat Dukan desserts and patisseries?

PP, PV and C at the top of the recipes indicate the phases of the Dukan Diet during which you can enjoy your desserts and patisseries.

The recipes fall into the following categories:
- Pure Protein Recipes: **PP**
- Protein + Vegetable Recipes: **PV**
- Consolidation Recipes: **C**

Foods that are classified as 'tolerated' (see opposite) are not allowed in Attack (phase 1) or on Thursdays during Consolidation and Stabilization (phases 3 and 4). (Please see *The Dukan Diet*, published in 2010, for a full explanation of my method.)

How much flavouring and sweetener should you use?

How powerful a flavouring is will vary according to which brand you are using, so don't worry if you want to change the quantity. Likewise, check your desserts and patisseries at the end of preparation to see if they are sweet enough for your liking and again, if necessary, vary the amount of sweetener you use.

Tolerated foods for desserts and patisseries

Tolerated foods are ingredients that let you add something special to your day-to-day cooking. They contain a little more fat and sugar than the foods you are allowed but eating them will not slow down your weight loss as long as you do not exceed two portions a day.

However, please note that tolerated foods are allowed only once you start your Cruise phase; they are not allowed in Attack (phase 1) or on your Pure Protein Thursdays (Consolidation and Stabilization).

TOLERATED FOODS

Fat-free fruit yoghurt	150g (5½oz)
Natural soya yoghurt	150g (5½oz)
Cornflour	1 tablespoon or 20g (¾oz)
Soya flour	1 tablespoon or 20g (¾oz)
3% fat max. crème fraîche	1 tablespoon or 30g (1oz)
11% fat sugar-free, fat-reduced cocoa powder	1 teaspoon or 7g
Wine for cooking (uncovered)	3 tablespoons or 30ml (1fl oz)
Soya milk	1 glass or 150ml (5fl oz)
Cheese – 7% fat max.	30g (1oz)
Oil	A few drops – then wipe away with kitchen paper
Ricoré chicory coffee	1 teaspoon or 7g
Sugar-free syrup	20ml (¾fl oz)
Goji berries	1–3 tablespoons, depending on the phase

Sweet Oat Bran Galettes

4 servings | **Preparation time: 5 minutes**
Cooking time: 10 minutes per galette

PP - PV

---

8 tablespoons oat bran
4 tablespoons wheat bran
8 tablespoons fat-free fromage frais
2 tablespoons Splenda granules
4 vanilla sticks Canderel
3 egg whites

- In a small bowl, combine all the ingredients except the egg whites and mix until smooth.

- Beat the egg whites until stiff and fold them into the mixture.

- Make the first galette by pouring a quarter of the mixture into a non-stick frying pan, warmed over a medium heat, and cook for about 5 minutes. Using a spatula, turn the galette over and cook for a further 5 minutes. Then make the other three galettes in the same way.

- To make chocolate galettes, add 1 teaspoon sugar-free fat-reduced cocoa powder to the galette mixture.

Maple Syrup Oat Bran Crêpes

4 servings | **Preparation time: 5 minutes**
Cooking time: 2–3 minutes per crêpe

PP - PV

---

2 tablespoons fat-free thick natural yoghurt
or natural soy yoghurt
2 eggs + 2 egg whites
4 tablespoons oat bran
2 tablespoons wheat bran
A little skimmed milk
4 tablespoons hot water
4 Canderel vanilla sticks
4 drops maple syrup flavouring

- Using a fork, stir together the yoghurt, whole eggs and egg whites in a bowl and beat for a few seconds.
- Add the oat and wheat brans and continue stirring the mixture.
- Depending on the texture of the yoghurt you are using, you may need to add a little skimmed milk if the mixture looks too thick.
- In the meantime, warm a non-stick frying pan over a medium heat. As soon as the pan is hot, pour in a small ladleful of the mixture and spread it out thinly so that the crêpe is not too thick. Cook for 1–2 minutes over a low heat, then carefully turn the crêpe over using a spatula and cook the other side. Repeat with the remaining mixture to make four crêpes.
- In a small bowl, mix together the hot water, vanilla sticks and maple syrup flavouring and pour over the crêpes. You can sprinkle over a little more sweetener if you wish.

Chocolate Freezer Crêpes

**4 servings | Preparation time: 20 minutes
Cooking time: 10 minutes | Freezing time: 1 hour**

PP - PV

4 tablespoons oat bran
12 tablespoons skimmed milk
2 eggs
3 tablespoons orange flower water
For the chocolate cream filling:
12 tablespoons skimmed milk
2 tablespoons cornflour
20 drops chocolate flavouring
4 teaspoons sugar-free fat-reduced cocoa powder
4 egg yolks
2 rounded tablespoons Splenda granules

■ To make the crêpes, mix together the oat bran, milk, eggs and orange flower water in a bowl. Wipe a non-stick frying pan with a drop of oil on some kitchen paper and warm over a medium heat. Pour in a quarter of the crêpe mixture, taking care to spread it out evenly – the crêpes need to be thin. Cook over a low heat for 1–2 minutes, then turn over using a spatula to cook the other side. Repeat with the remaining mixture.

■ To make the chocolate cream filling, mix a little of the skimmed milk with the cornflour to form a paste. Heat the rest of the milk in a saucepan with the chocolate flavouring and cocoa powder. In a bowl, stir the egg yolks into the sweetener and then add the cornflour paste. Gradually pour in the hot milk, stirring all the time with a wooden spoon. Return the mixture to the saucepan and cook for 3 minutes, stirring continually, then leave to cool.

■ Place each crêpe on a sheet of clingfilm. Spread the cold chocolate cream over the crêpes then roll them up, twisting the clingfilm at each end to secure tightly. Freeze the rolls for 1 hour. Take out of the freezer, remove the clingfilm and serve immediately.

Light Lemon-lime Waffles

4 servings | **Preparation time: 10 minutes**
Cooking time: will vary according to the waffle machine

PP - PV

---

2 eggs + 4 egg whites
Pinch of salt
4 tablespoons cornflour
1 × 7g sachet dried yeast
4 tablespoons fat-free fromage frais
2 tablespoons Splenda granules
1 tablespoon sugar-free lemon-lime syrup (e.g. Teisseire)*

■ In a bowl, beat the egg whites with the salt until stiff.

■ Combine the whole eggs with the rest of the ingredients in another bowl. Once the mixture is nice and smooth, gently fold in the stiffly beaten egg whites.

■ Warm the waffle machine and wipe the metal plates with some lightly oiled kitchen paper.

■ When the machine is ready, make your waffles.

* You can also use lemon, lime or meringue pie flavourings.

Dukan Langues de Chat

4 servings | **Preparation time: 15 minutes**
Cooking time: 15–20 minutes

PP - PV

---

3 tablespoons Splenda granules
4 tablespoons cornflour
1 teaspoon dried yeast
150g (5½oz) fat-free natural yoghurt
5 drops melted butter flavouring
10 drops vanilla flavouring
6 egg whites
Pinch of salt

- Preheat the oven to 180°C/350°F/Gas 4 and line a baking sheet with greaseproof paper.
- In a bowl, combine the sweetener, cornflour, yeast, yoghurt and flavourings.
- In another bowl, beat the egg whites with the salt until very stiff and fold into the yoghurt mixture.
- Pour the mixture into a piping bag and squeeze out finger biscuits about 8cm (3¼in) long on to the baking sheet. Bake in the preheated oven for 15–20 minutes, keeping a careful eye on the biscuits to check when they are ready.

Orange Flower Madeleines

4 servings | **Preparation time: 15 minutes plus 30–60 minutes resting**
Cooking time: 15–20 minutes

PP - PV

---

8 eggs
8 tablespoons Splenda granules
12 tablespoons fat-free fromage frais
12 tablespoons oat bran
8 tablespoons cornflour
2 × 8g sachets baking powder
4 tablespoons orange flower water

- Preheat the oven to 180°C/350°F/Gas 4.
- In a bowl, whisk together the eggs and the sweetener until you have a creamy white mixture.
- Gradually stir in the fromage frais, oat bran and cornflour mixed with the baking powder. Add the orange flower water and keep stirring until the mixture is nice and smooth.
- Leave to rest for 30–60 minutes.
- Pour the mixture into a non-stick madeleine tin and bake in the preheated oven for 15–20 minutes, keeping a careful eye on the madeleines.
- Leave the madeleines to cool in the tin before turning them out. They will keep for several days in an airtight container.

Chocolate Cookies

4 servings | **Preparation time: 10 minutes**
Cooking time: 15–20 minutes

PP - PV

---

8 eggs, separated
8 tablespoons oat bran
4 tablespoons wheat bran
2 tablespoons Splenda granules
4 teaspoons sugar-free fat-reduced cocoa powder
2 tablespoons vanilla flavouring
Pinch of salt

- Preheat the oven to 180°C/350°F/Gas 4 and line a baking sheet with greaseproof paper.

- In a bowl, combine the egg yolks, oat and wheat brans, sweetener, cocoa powder and vanilla flavouring.

- In a separate bowl, beat the egg whites with the salt until very stiff, then gently fold them into the bran mixture.

- Spoon the mixture in small rounds on to the baking sheet and bake in the preheated oven for 15–20 minutes. Keep a careful eye on the cookies, checking to see when they are ready.

Pistachio Sponge Fingers

4 servings | **Preparation time 10: minutes**
Cooking time: 5–10 minutes

PP - PV

---

8 egg whites
Pinch of salt
4 tablespoons wheat bran
8 tablespoons oat bran
4 tablespoons fat-free fromage frais
4 tablespoons cornflour
4 teaspoons pistachio flavouring
12 drops melted butter flavouring
12 drops bitter almond flavouring
6 tablespoons Hermesetas granulated sweetener
12 drops green food colouring (optional)

- Preheat the oven to 180°C/350°F/Gas 4.
- In a bowl, beat the egg whites with the salt until stiff.
- In another bowl, mix together the brans, fromage frais, cornflour, flavourings, sweetener and food colouring (if using). Gradually fold in the beaten egg whites.
- Pour the mixture into a silicone sponge finger mould. Lower the oven temperature to 150°C/300°F/Gas 2 and bake for 5–10 minutes. Keep a careful eye on the sponge fingers, checking to see when they are ready.

Muffins

6 servings | **Preparation time: 10 minutes**
Cooking time: 30 minutes

PP - PV

---

4 eggs, separated
12 tablespoons oat bran
4 tablespoons fat-free fromage frais
1 tablespoon liquid Hermesetas
½ × 7g sachet dried yeast
Flavour of your choice: grated zest of 1 unwaxed lemon (PV only),
1 teaspoon ground cinnamon, 1 tablespoon coffee,
4 teaspoons sugar-free fat-reduced cocoa powder,
1 tablespoon pistachio flavouring, 1 tablespoon orange
flavouring, etc.

- Preheat the oven to 180°C/350°F/Gas 4.
- In a bowl, beat the egg whites until stiff.
- In another bowl, mix together the egg yolks, oat bran, fromage frais, sweetener and yeast, then gently fold in the stiffly beaten egg whites. Finally add the flavour or flavouring of your choice.
- Pour the mixture into silicone muffin moulds and bake in the preheated oven for 20–30 minutes, keeping a careful eye on the muffins to check when they are ready.

Butternut Squash Muffins

6 servings | **Preparation time: 30 minutes**
Cooking time: 30–40 minutes

PV

---

9 tablespoons oat bran
1 × 8g sachet baking powder
6 level tablespoons Splenda granules
3 tablespoons powdered skimmed milk
Generous pinch of ground cinnamon
200g (7oz) grated butternut squash
Freshly grated nutmeg
4 tablespoons fat-free fromage frais
4 eggs
2 teaspoons rum flavouring

- Preheat the oven to 230°C/450°F/Gas 8 and remove the oven shelf.

- In a bowl, mix together the oat bran, baking powder, sweetener, powdered skimmed milk, cinnamon, butternut squash and nutmeg. Combine all the ingredients and then add the fromage frais, eggs and rum flavouring, stirring together thoroughly.

- Pour the mixture into a silicone muffin tin lined with paper cases. Replace the shelf in the middle of the oven and lower the temperature to 180°C/350°F/Gas 4. Bake the muffins for 30–40 minutes, keeping a careful eye on them. Leave the muffins to cool completely before turning them out of the tin.

Oat Bran Biscuits

4 servings | **Preparation time: 10 minutes**
Cooking time: 15 minutes

PP - PV

---

8 eggs, separated
1 tablespoon vanilla flavouring
10 drops melted butter flavouring
1 teaspoon liquid Hermesetas
8 tablespoons fat-free fromage frais
8 tablespoons oat bran

- Preheat the oven to 150°C/300°F/Gas 2.

- In a bowl, combine the egg yolks, vanilla flavouring, butter flavouring, sweetener, fromage frais and oat bran.

- In another bowl, beat the egg whites until stiff. Gently fold them into the bran mixture.

- Pour the mixture into a silicone macaroon mould and bake for 15 minutes, keeping a careful eye on the biscuits to check when they are ready.

Mocha Meringues

Makes around 12 meringues | Preparation time: 10 minutes
Cooking time: 15–20 minutes

PP - PV

---

3 egg whites
Pinch of salt
2 teaspoons sugar-free fat-reduced cocoa powder
6 tablespoons Splenda granules
30ml very strong coffee

- Preheat the oven to 150°C/300°F/Gas 2 and line a baking sheet with greaseproof paper.
- In a bowl, beat the egg whites with the salt until very stiff.
- Add the cocoa powder to the sweetener and sprinkle over the egg whites, then add the coffee. Continue beating the egg whites for about 30 seconds.
- Arrange small heaps of the mixture on the baking sheet and bake in the oven for 15–20 minutes, checking carefully to see when the meringues are ready.

Speculoos Biscuits

2 servings | **Preparation time: 15 minutes**
Cooking time: 20 minutes

PP - PV

---

6 tablespoons oat bran
2 eggs
2 rounded tablespoons Splenda granules
2 tablespoons cornflour
40 drops speculoos flavouring*

- Preheat the oven to 180°C/350°F/Gas 4 and line a baking sheet with greaseproof paper.
- Blend all the ingredients. Using a piping bag, shape the mixture into finger biscuits on to the baking sheet.
- Bake the biscuits in the preheated oven for 20 minutes, keeping a careful eye on them. When they are ready, turn off the oven and leave them to cool in the oven with the door closed.

* Speculoos is a lightly spiced Dutch biscuit. You can replace the speculoos flavouring with a pinch of mixed spice or a mix of whatever spices you have, such as cinnamon, nutmeg, ginger and cardamon.

Coconut Rock Cakes

4 servings | **Preparation time: 10 minutes**
Cooking time: 15 minutes

PP - PV

---

8 tablespoons oat bran
4 tablespoons wheat bran
30 drops coconut flavouring
2 teaspoons liquid Hermesetas
8 eggs, separated
Pinch of salt

- Preheat the oven to 200°C/400°F/Gas 6 and line a baking sheet with greaseproof paper.
- In a bowl, combine the oat and wheat brans, flavouring, sweetener and egg yolks.
- In another bowl, beat the egg whites with the salt until stiff.
- Add the beaten egg whites to the bran mixture little by little until it has a fairly compact consistency.
- Shape the mixture into four cakes and arrange them on the baking sheet. Bake in the preheated oven for 15 minutes, keeping a careful eye on the rock cakes to check when they are ready.

Hazelnut Macaroons

4 servings | **Preparation time: 5 minutes**
Cooking time: 15 minutes

PP - PV

---

4 egg whites
Pinch of salt
4 tablespoons Splenda granules
8 tablespoons oat bran, plus extra for sprinkling
1 teaspoon hazelnut flavouring

- Preheat the oven to 150°C/300°F/Gas 2 and line a baking sheet with greaseproof paper.
- In a bowl, beat the egg whites with the salt until very stiff.
- In a separate bowl, mix together the sweetener, oat bran and hazelnut flavouring. Carefully fold the beaten egg whites into the bran mixture.
- Fill a piping bag with the mixture and pipe small, round macaroon shapes on to the baking sheet. Sprinkle over some oat bran and bake in the preheated oven for 15 minutes, keeping a careful eye on the macaroons to check when they are ready.

Amaretti Biscuits

4 servings | **Preparation time: 15 minutes**
Cooking time: 20 minutes

PP - PV

---

3 egg whites
Pinch of salt
6 tablespoons Splenda granules
8 tablespoons oat bran
2 teaspoons bitter almond flavouring (or to taste)

- Preheat the oven to 200°C/400°F/Gas 6 and line a baking sheet with greaseproof paper.
- In a bowl, beat the egg white with the salt until very stiff. While still beating the egg white, sprinkle in the sweetener until you have a sort of thick, sticky meringue mixture.
- Fold the oat bran into the egg white mixture and add the flavouring. Stir thoroughly.
- Use two tablespoons to shape eight small balls about 3cm (1¼in) in diameter and place them on the baking sheet.
- Bake in the preheated oven for 20 minutes, keeping a careful eye on the biscuits. They should be crunchy on the outside but chewy inside. Leave them to cool completely before serving.

Orange Custard Flan

4 servings | Preparation time: 10 minutes
Cooking time: 30 minutes

PP - PV

---

8 tablespoons fat-free fromage frais
2 eggs
3 tablespoons Splenda granules
6 tablespoons cornflour
½ × 8g sachet baking powder
1 tablespoon orange flower water
Grated zest of 1 orange (unwaxed if possible)
4 tablespoons powdered skimmed milk

- Preheat the oven to 160°C/325°F/Gas 3.

- Combine all the ingredients together in a bowl, stirring very thoroughly to get as smooth a mixture as possible.

- Pour the mixture into a 18cm (7in) flan dish.

- Place in the preheated oven and bake for 30 minutes, keeping a careful eye on the flan to check when it is ready.

Coffee and Hazelnut Swiss Roll

4 servings | Preparation time: 20 minutes
Cooking time: 15–20 minutes

PP - PV

For the sponge:
3 eggs, separated
8 tablespoons cornflour
10 drops vanilla flavouring
Pinch of salt
2 tablespoons Splenda granules
For the filling:
2 egg whites
Pinch of salt
30g (1oz) virtually fat-free quark
30g (1oz) fat-free fromage frais
2 tablespoons Splenda granules
2 teaspoons instant coffee granules (e.g. Nescafé)
10 drops hazelnut flavouring

- Preheat the oven to 180°C/350°F/Gas 4.

- To make the sponge, whisk together the egg yolks and the cornflour in a bowl, and add the vanilla flavouring. In another bowl, beat the egg whites with the salt until stiff and add the sweetener. Carefully fold the beaten egg whites into the egg yolk mixture.

- Tip the sponge mixture into a 33 x 22cm (12 x 8in) rectangular ovenproof dish and spread out evenly. Bake in the preheated oven for 15–20 minutes, keeping a careful eye on the sponge.

- To make the filling, beat the egg whites with the salt until stiff. In a separate bowl, stir together the quark, fromage frais and sweetener, then add the coffee powder and hazelnut flavouring. Gently fold in the beaten egg whites.

- Once the sponge is cooked, leave to cool before spreading over the filling and rolling up very carefully. Refrigerate before serving.

Light Lemony Sponge Cake

2 servings | Preparation time: 10 minutes
Cooking time: 20 minutes

PP - PV

---

4 eggs, separated
4 tablespoons Splenda granules
Grated zest of 1 lemon
40g (1½oz) cornflour

- Preheat the oven to 180°C/350°F/Gas 4 and line a 18cm (7in) cake tin with greaseproof paper.

- In a bowl, beat the egg whites until stiff.

- In another bowl, combine the egg yolks and sweetener, then add the lemon zest and cornflour. Carefully fold in the beaten egg whites.

- Pour the mixture into the cake tin and bake in the preheated oven for 20 minutes, keeping a careful eye on the sponge. It is ready once it turns golden brown on top.

Gingerbread

4 servings | Preparation time: 10 minutes
Cooking time: 45 minutes

PP - PV

---

8 tablespoons oat bran
4 tablespoons wheat bran
3 tablespoons powdered skimmed milk
1 × 8g sachet baking powder
6 tablespoons fat-free fromage frais
3 eggs + 3 egg whites
1½ teaspoons liquid Hermesetas
20 drops gingerbread flavouring or 2 tablespoons
gingerbread spice mixture (ground cinnamon, star anise,
nutmeg, ginger, cloves)

- Preheat the oven to 180°C/350°F/Gas 4 and lightly grease 20cm (8in) loaf tin using some oiled kitchen paper.

- In a bowl, mix together the oat and wheat brans, powdered milk and baking powder. Add the fromage frais and stir well. Next add the whole eggs and the egg whites. Stir until the mixture is nice and smooth. Finish off by stirring in the sweetener and flavouring or spices.

- Pour the mixture into the ovenproof dish and bake in the preheated oven for 45 minutes. To check that the cake is done, insert the tip of a knife, which should come out clean.

Yoghurt Cake

2 servings | Preparation time: 15 minutes
Cooking time: 35 minutes

PP - PV

---

4 tablespoons oat bran
5 eggs
150g (5½oz) fat-free natural (or flavoured) yoghurt
6 tablespoons powdered skimmed milk
2 tablespoons Splenda granules
1 × 7g sachet dried yeast
Flavouring of your choice (e.g. hazelnut, vanilla,
orange flower water)

- Preheat the oven to 200°C/400°F/Gas 6 and line a 20cm (8in) loaf tin with greaseproof paper.
- Process the oat bran as finely as possible using a blender or food processor and then combine with all the other ingredients.
- Transfer the mixture to tin. Reduce the oven temperature to 180°C/350°F/Gas 4 and bake for 35 minutes until lightly golden on top.

Carrot Cake

2 servings | Preparation time: 25 minutes
Cooking time: 45 minutes

PV

---

3 eggs, separated
2 teaspoons liquid Hermesetas
1 teaspoon ground cinnamon
1 teaspoon rum flavouring
4 tablespoons oat bran
1 teaspoon dried yeast
250g (9oz) carrots, finely grated
Grated zest of 1 lemon

- Preheat the oven to 180°C/350°F/Gas 4 and line a 20cm (8in) loaf tin with greaseproof paper.
- In a bowl, mix together the egg yolks and sweetener.
- Add the cinnamon, rum flavouring, oat bran and yeast. Then mix in the grated carrots and lemon zest.
- In another bowl, beat the egg whites until very stiff and gently fold them into the carrot mixture, which should be quite runny.
- Pour the mixture into the tin and bake in the preheated oven for 45 minutes, checking the cake at regular intervals.

Excellentissime

**2 servings | Preparation time: 10 minutes
Cooking time: 30 minutes**

PP - PV

---

6 tablespoons oat bran
5 eggs
3 tablespoons fat-free fromage frais
6 tablespoons powdered skimmed milk
2 tablespoons Splenda granules
1 × 7g sachet dried yeast
4 teaspoons sugar-free fat-reduced cocoa powder
10 drops bitter almond flavouring
10 drops hazelnut flavouring

- Preheat the oven to 200°C/400°F/Gas 6 and line a 20cm (8in) loaf tin with greseproof paper.
- Stir together all the ingredients very thoroughly in a bowl.
- Pour the mixture into the tin and bake in the preheated oven for about 30 minutes.

Chocolate and Pear Marble Cake

2 servings | Preparation time: 10 minutes
Cooking time: 45 minutes

PP - PV

---

6 eggs, separated
6 tablespoons Splenda granules
20 drops melted butter flavouring
10 tablespoons fat-free fromage frais
2 tablespoons cornflour
2 teaspoons baking powder
2 doses protein powder (such as Protifar or Nesvital)
Pinch of salt
2 teaspoons sugar-free fat-reduced cocoa powder
20 drops pear flavouring

- Preheat the oven to 180°C/350°F/Gas 4.

- In a bowl, mix together the egg yolks, sweetener, melted butter flavouring and fromage frais. Add the cornflour, baking powder and protein powder.

- In another bowl, beat the egg whites with the salt until very stiff, then gently fold them into the fromage frais mixture.

- Divide the mixture between two bowls. Add the cocoa powder to the first bowl and the pear flavouring to the other.

- Pour both mixtures into a muffin tin mould, alternating the layers to create a marbled effect, and bake in the preheated oven for 15–20 minutes, keeping a careful eye on the cake to check when it is ready.

Orange Flower Bran Brioches

2 servings | **Preparation time: 15 minutes**
Cooking time: 10–15 minutes

PP - PV

---

4 tablespoons oat bran
2 tablespoons wheat bran
4 tablespoons cornflour
1 teaspoon baking powder
4 eggs
4 tablespoons Splenda granules
8 tablespoons fat-free fromage frais
10 drops melted butter flavouring
1 tablespoon orange flower water

- Preheat the oven to 180°C/350°F/Gas 4.

- Process the oat and wheat brans as finely as possible using a blender or food processor.

- Mix together the cornflour, brans and baking powder. Next add the eggs along with the sweetener, fromage frais, butter flavouring and orange flower water, and stir everything together very thoroughly.

- Pour the mixture into silicone brioche moulds and bake in the preheated oven for 10–15 minutes. Keep a careful eye on the brioches to check when they are ready, and then turn the oven off and leave them to cool in the oven with the door closed.

Lemon Extravaganza

2 servings | Preparation time: 20 minutes
Refrigeration time: 2 hours minimum

PP - PV

---

2 gelatine leaves
Juice of 4 lemons
Grated zest of 1 unwaxed lemon
100g (3½oz) fat-free fromage frais
2 tablespoons crystallized stevia
2 egg whites
Pinch of salt

- Soak the gelatine in a little cold water.

- Warm the lemon juice and zest in a small saucepan. Drain the gelatine leaves and add to the pan and stir until the gelatine has dissolved. Add the fromage frais and sweetener and mix well.

- In a bowl, beat the egg whites with the salt until stiff and gently fold them into the mixture.

- Pour the mixture into a bavarois mould and refrigerate for at least 2 hours before serving.

Praline Bavarois

4 servings | Preparation time: 20 minutes
Refrigeration time: 2 hours minimum

PP - PV

---

4 gelatine leaves
1 teaspoon vanilla flavouring
6 Canderel vanilla sticks
4 egg whites
Pinch of salt
400g (14oz) fat-free fromage frais
40 drops hazelnut flavouring

- Soak the gelatine in a little cold water.

- Warm a little water in the bottom of a small saucepan and add the vanilla flavouring and then the drained gelatine. Once the gelatine has dissolved, remove the pan from the heat. Next add the vanilla sticks.

- Beat the egg whites with the salt until stiff and then add the gelatine syrup to the egg whites, whisking continuously. Add the fromage frais and then the hazelnut flavouring.

- Pour the mixture into a bavarois mould and refrigerate for at least 2 hours before serving.

Vanilla Tart

4 servings | Preparation time: 10 minutes
Cooking time: 40 minutes

PP - PV

---

6 tablespoons oat bran
6 tablespoons fat-free fromage frais
6 eggs
150g (5½oz) sugar-free, fat-free, vanilla-flavoured
yoghurt (e.g. Sveltesse)
1 tablespoon vanilla flavouring
2 tablespoons orange flower water
2 teaspoons liquid Hermesetas

- Preheat the oven to 200°C/400°F/Gas 6.

- In a large bowl, thoroughly combine all the ingredients and then pour the mixture into a 18cm (7in) silicone tart mould.

- Bake in the preheated oven for 20–25 minutes, keeping a careful eye on the tart to check when it is ready.

Lemon Meringue Pie

4 servings | Preparation time: 15 minutes
Cooking time: 35–40 minutes

PP - PV

For the galette base:
2 egg whites
4 tablespoons oat bran
2 tablespoons wheat bran
1 tablespoon Splenda granules
4 tablespoons fat-free fromage frais
For the filling:
200ml (7fl oz) water
4 eggs
2 tablespoons cornflour
8 tablespoons Splenda granules
2 teaspoons lemon meringue pie flavouring
2 egg whites
Pinch of salt
A few small slices of lime, to decorate

- Preheat the oven to 200°C/400°F/Gas 6.

- Prepare the galette base by beating the egg whites until stiff and combining them with the remaining ingredients. Use this mixture to line the bottom of a 21cm (8in) pie dish.

- Blind - bake the galette base in the preheated oven for 5–10 minutes.

- To make the filling, heat the water in a saucepan.

- In a bowl, combine the whole eggs, cornflour, 7 tablespoons of the sweetener and the lemon meringue pie flavouring.

- Pour this mixture into the saucepan, warm it over a gentle heat and stir carefully until it thickens. Then pour the lemon mixture over the galette base.

- Lower the oven temperature to 180°C/350°F/Gas 4 and bake the pie for 20 minutes. Remove from the oven and leave to cool slightly.

- In a bowl, beat the egg whites with the salt and the remaining tablespoon of sweetener until quite stiff. Using a piping bag, decorate the top of the pie with the egg whites.

- Return the pie to the oven for a further 10 minutes until the meringue topping turns golden brown. Decorate with slices of lime.

Triple Chocolate Tartlets

**4 servings | Preparation time: 15 minutes | Cooking time: 10 minutes
Refrigeration time: 2 hours minimum**

PP - PV

For the tartlet bases:
3 eggs, separated
Pinch of salt
1 teaspoon liquid Hermesetas
1 tablespoon cornflour
10 drops dark chocolate
flavouring

For the filling:
7 tablespoons powdered
skimmed milk
1 tablespoon sugar-free
fat-reduced cocoa powder
4 Canderel vanilla sticks
1½ egg yolks
5 drops hazelnut flavouring
3 tablespoons skimmed milk
5 drops white chocolate
flavouring

■ Preheat the oven to 150°C/300°F/Gas 2. In a bowl, beat the egg whites with the salt until very stiff. Add the sweetener and continue beating the egg whites for a few minutes. In another bowl, combine the egg yolks with the cornflour. Add the dark chocolate flavouring and stir vigorously into the yolks. Gently fold in the egg whites. Carefully roll the mixture out over a square baking sheet, ensuring that there will be enough to line the base of four small tartlet dishes. Bake in the oven for 10 minutes, keeping a careful eye on it to make sure it does not overcook. Remove from the oven and turn out on to your work top. Cut out bases and place in four small tartlet dishes.

■ To make the filling, mix together 5 tablespoons of the powdered skimmed milk, the cocoa powder, 3 of the vanilla sticks, 1 egg yolk, the hazelnut flavouring and 2 tablespoons of the skimmed milk. Whisk the mixture vigorously and then put to one side. In a separate bowl, combine the remaining 2 tablespoons powdered skimmed milk, vanilla stick, ½ egg yolk, 1 tablespoon skimmed milk and the white chocolate flavouring. Again, beat vigorously and put to one side. Pour the cocoa mixture into the tartlet dishes, then pour over a few drops of the white chocolate mixture. Use a wooden cocktail stick to create a marbled pattern. Refrigerate the tartlets for at least 2 hours before serving.

Chocolate Chestnut Tart

**4 servings | Preparation time: 15 minutes
Cooking time: 20 minutes**

PP - PV

For the tart base:
6 tablespoons oat bran
2 eggs
2 tablespoons fat-free fromage frais
1 teaspoon vanilla flavouring
For the filling:
4 teaspoons sugar-free fat-reduced cocoa powder
4 eggs
1 teaspoon liquid Hermesetas
1 teaspoon marron glacé flavouring
4 tablespoons 3% fat crème fraîche

- Preheat the oven to 230°C/450°F/Gas 8.

- In a bowl, mix together all the ingredients for the tart base. Pour into a 21cm (8in) tart tin or two 8cm (3.5in) tins and bake in the preheated oven for about 10 minutes, keeping a careful eye on the base to check that it is not overcooked.

- To make the chocolate and chestnut filling, combine all the ingredients in a bowl and beat vigorously until you have a nice smooth paste.

- Remove the tart base from the oven and pour over the filling. Bake for a further 10 minutes or so, keeping a careful eye on the tart to check when it is ready.

Strawberry Tartlets

4 servings | Preparation time: 15 minutes
Cooking time: 15 minutes | Refrigeration time: 2 hours minimum

PP - PV

For the tartlet bases:
2 tablespoons oat bran
6 doses protein powder (such as Protifar or Nesvital)
1 egg white
30g (1oz) fat-free fromage frais
30g (1oz) virtually fat-free quark
2 tablespoons Splenda granules
For the strawberry cream filling:
2 egg yolks
2 tablespoons Splenda granules
1 tablespoon protein powder (such as Protifar or Nesvital)
150ml (5fl oz) skimmed milk
25 drops strawberry tart flavouring

- Preheat the oven to 180°C/350°F/Gas 4.

- Prepare the tartlet bases by mixing together all the ingredients. Roll out the pastry and use to line four tartlet tins. Bake in the preheated oven for 15 minutes, keeping a careful eye on the bases to check when they are ready. Remove from the oven and leave to cool.

- To make the cream filling, mix together the egg yolks, sweetener and protein powder. In a saucepan, heat the milk and strawberry flavouring for a few minutes and then add the protein mixture. Stir continuously over a gentle heat until the mixture thickens.

- Divide the cream between the four baked tartlet bases and refrigerate for at least 2 hours before serving.

Fromage Frais Gâteau

4 servings | **Preparation time: 10 minutes**
Cooking time: 30 minutes | **Refrigeration time: 2 hours minimum**

PP - PV

125g (4½ oz) fat-free fromage frais
2 tablespoons cornflour
½ × 8g sachet baking powder
Grated zest of 1 unwaxed lemon
2 teaspoons liquid Hermesetas
2 eggs, separated + 2 egg whites
Pinch of salt

- Preheat the oven to 200°C/400°F/Gas 6.
- In a bowl, combine all the ingredients except for the egg white and salt.
- In a separate bowl, whisk the 4 egg whites with the salt until very stiff.
- Gradually fold the beaten egg whites into the fromage frais mixture. Pour into a 18cm (7in) tin and bake in the preheated oven for 30 minutes.
- When the gâteau has cooled, refrigerate it for at least 2 hours. It should be served cold.

Morello Cherry and Pistachio Mini Cheesecakes

4 servings | Preparation time: 30 minutes
Cooking time: 60 minutes | Refrigeration time: 4 hours minimum

PP - PV

For the biscuit bases:
4 tablespoons oat bran
2 tablespoons wheat bran
10 drops vanilla flavouring
1 tablespoon Splenda granules
2 egg yolks
2 tablespoons skimmed milk
For the cheesecake:
2 eggs, separated
2 teaspoons liquid Hermesetas
1 teaspoon pistachio flavouring

1 tablespoon cornflour
1 × 2g sachet agar-agar
500g (1lb 2oz) fat-free
fromage frais
Pinch of salt
For the morello cherry topping:
200ml (7fl oz) water
1 × 2g sachet agar-agar
1½ teaspoons liquid Hermesetas
1 teaspoon morello
cherry flavouring

- Preheat the oven to 180°C/350°F/Gas 4. First make the biscuit bases. In a bowl, mix together the oat and wheat brans, vanilla flavouring and sweetener. Add the egg yolks, mix thoroughly, then pour in the milk, stirring all the time. Pour the mixture into four individual ramekin dishes and bake in the oven for 15 minutes, keeping a careful eye on the bases to check when they are ready.

- To make the cheesecake, vigorously stir together the egg yolks with the sweetener, pistachio flavouring, cornflour and agar-agar. Add the fromage frais. In a separate bowl, beat the egg whites with the salt until stiff, then gently fold into the fromage frais mixture. Pour over the cooked biscuit bases. Bake the ramekins in the preheated oven for 40 minutes, keeping a careful eye on them. Remove from the oven and leave to cool. Refrigerate for at least 4 hours (or, even better, overnight).

- To make the morello cherry topping, stir all the ingredients together in a saucepan and bring to the boil. Leave to cool for a few minutes, then pour over the mini cheesecakes and put them back in the fridge until ready to serve.

Coffee and Cinnamon Granita

2 servings | Preparation time: 10 minutes
Freezing/refrigeration time: 1¼ hours

PP - PV

500ml (18fl oz) hot black coffee
4 Canderel vanilla sticks
1 teaspoon ground cinnamon
3 cardamom seeds

■ Mix together the hot coffee, sweetener and spices. Stir thoroughly and leave to cool.

■ Pour the mixture into a shallow freezer-proof bowl and place in the freezer for about 1 hour.

■ Take the bowl out of the freezer, and put the mixture through a blender for 1 minute. Divide the granita between two large glass dishes and place in the fridge for a further 15 minutes before serving.

Italian-style Strawberry Ice Cream

2 servings | **Preparation time: 15 minutes**
Freezing time: 2½ hours minimum

PP - PV

---

3 eggs, separated
Pinch of salt
90g (3¼oz) fat-free fromage frais
40g (1½oz) virtually fat-free quark
2 tablespoons low-fat single cream
1 teaspoon crystallized stevia
1 teaspoon strawberry flavouring
(or any other flavouring of your choice)

- In a bowl, beat the egg whites with the salt until stiff.

- In a separate bowl, combine the egg yolks, fromage frais, quark, low-fat cream, sweetener and strawberry flavouring.

- Gently fold the beaten egg whites into the mixture. Check that it is sufficiently sweet for your taste.

- Transfer the mixture to two large, pretty, freezer-proof dishes and freeze for at least 2½ hours.

Vanilla Lollipops

4 servings | Preparation time: 10 minutes
Freezing time: overnight

PP - PV

---

2 teaspoons vanilla flavouring
300g (10½ oz) fat-free fromage frais
4 Canderel vanilla sticks

- Have ready four plastic lollipop moulds with sticks.
- Stir the vanilla flavouring into the fromage frais.
- Add the sweetener and beat the mixture using an electric whisk.
- Fill the lollipop moulds and freeze overnight.
- Enjoy them on the following day!

Sabayon Ice Cream

4 servings | **Preparation time: 15 minutes**
Freezing time: overnight

PP - PV

---

3 eggs, separated
4 tablespoons Canderel granules
1 tablespoon vanilla flavouring
1 tablespoon orange flower water
1 teaspoon oil

- Place four small ramekins in the freezer.
- In a bowl, beat the egg whites until stiff.
- In another bowl, stir together the egg yolks, sweetener, vanilla flavouring and orange flower water until the mixture becomes frothy. Drizzle in the oil and beat the mixture as if making a sweet mayonnaise.
- Gently fold the beaten egg whites into the mixture and check it is sweet enough for your taste.
- Divide the mixture between the frozen ramekin dishes and place them in the freezer overnight.

Jasmine Tea Granita

4 servings | **Preparation time: 5 minutes**
Cooking time: 10 minutes | **Freezing time: 2 hours**

PP - PV

---

1 litre (1¾ pints) water
Grated zest of 1 unwaxed lemon
1 tablespoon jasmine tea leaves
2 teaspoons crystallized stevia

- Bring the water and lemon zest to the boil in a large pan. Add the tea and leave to infuse for 8 minutes.
- Pass the liquid through a small conical strainer and add the sweetener. Check that it is sweet enough for your taste before pouring into a large freezer-proof dish and placing in the freezer.
- After an hour, stir the mixture to break up any ice crystals that are starting to appear. Put back in the freezer for another hour or so, to allow the granita to form.
- The granita will turn into a crumbly block that is best broken up using a fork. Spoon into four glass dishes and serve.

Lemon and Lime Sorbet

4 servings | **Preparation time: 10 minutes**
Freezing time: 4 hours

PP - PV

---

2 unwaxed limes
2 unwaxed lemons
500g (1lb 2oz) fat-free fromage frais
3 teaspoons crystallized stevia

- You will need an ice-cream maker for this dish.
- Finely blend the zest of 1of the limes. Add the fromage frais, the juice from all the limes and lemons and the sweetener to the blender and blend thoroughly.
- Pour the mixture into a freezer-proof dish and freeze for 4 hours before churning in the ice-cream maker for 5 minutes.

Caribbean Coconut Sorbet

**4 servings | Preparation time: 20 minutes
Ice-cream maker: 30 minutes**

PP - PV

3 egg yolks
1 tablespoon liquid Hermesetas
1 teaspoon ground cinnamon
Pinch of grated nutmeg
Grated zest of 1 unwaxed lemon
1 teaspoon orange flower water
5 drops melted butter flavouring
1 teaspoon coconut flavouring
10 drops rum flavouring
300ml (10fl oz) skimmed milk
3 tablespoons fat-free fromage frais
2 × 2g sachets agar-agar

- You will need an ice-cream maker for this dish.
- In a small bowl, combine the egg yolks, sweetener, cinnamon, nutmeg, lemon zest, orange flower water and flavourings. Beat the ingredients together for a few minutes with an electric whisk.
- Add half the milk and the fromage frais to the mixture, and stir everything together thoroughly. Put to one side.
- Bring the remaining milk to the boil in a saucepan, then add the agar-agar and stir well. Continue stirring for a few minutes before removing from the heat.
- Add this hot milk very gradually to the coconut mixture, stirring all the time. Pour the mixture into the ice-cream maker and leave to churn for about 30 minutes, until it hardens. Remove the ice cream from the machine and serve straightaway.

Ices

Banana Split

4 servings | Preparation time: 35 minutes
Refrigeration time: overnight

PP - PV

---

4 gelatine leaves
8 tablespoons fat-free fromage frais
2 teaspoons banana flavouring
30 drops yellow food colouring
3 tablespoons Canderel granules
60ml (2¼fl oz) skimmed milk
2 eggs, separated
Salt
3 tablespoons virtually fat-free quark

3 Canderel vanilla sticks
1 teaspoon vanilla flavouring
1 teaspoon strawberry flavouring
30 drops red food colouring
(optional)
4 teaspoons sugar-free fat-reduced
cocoa powder
1 teaspoon hazelnut flavouring

- Soften the gelatine leaves in a bowl of cold water.

- In a separate small bowl, combine 5 tablespoons of the fromage frais with the banana flavouring, yellow colouring and granulated sweetener. Remove the gelatine from the water and wring dry. Heat the skimmed milk in a small saucepan, add the gelatine and dissolve. Add the warm milk to the banana mixture and leave to set in the fridge overnight.

- Beat 1 of the egg whites with a pinch of salt until very stiff. Mix together 2 tablespoons each of the quark and remaining fromage frais with 2 of the vanilla sticks and add 1 of the egg yolks. Divide the mixture between two freezer containers, adding vanilla flavouring to one and strawberry flavouring and red colouring (if using) to the other. Divide the beaten egg white between the two mixtures, combine well and place them in the freezer to set.

- To make a chocolate sauce, mix together the remaining egg yolk with the cocoa powder, remaining vanilla stick and a few drops of hazelnut flavouring.

- Beat the remaining egg white with a pinch of salt until stiff and gently fold in 1 tablespoon each of the remaining sweetened quark and fromage frais to make a Dukan Chantilly (see page 172).

- When ready to serve, use a melon baller to scoop small balls of banana ice cream and arrange them in glass dishes. Then add scoops of each of the other two ice-cream flavours and finish with a tablespoon of the chocolate sauce and some Dukan Chantilly on top.

Dukan Violet and Strawberry Marshmallows

2 servings | Preparation time: 15 minutes
Refrigeration time: 1 hour minimum

PP - PV

---

8 gelatine leaves
6 egg whites
Pinch of salt
150ml (5fl oz) water
6 tablespoons Canderel granules
15 drops violet flavouring
15 drops strawberry flavouring

- Soften the gelatine in a bowl of water.
- In another bowl, beat the egg whites with the salt until very stiff. Divide the beaten egg whites into two portions.
- Dissolve half the gelatine in half the measured water in a small saucepan over a gentle heat. Add 3 tablespoons
of the sweetener and the violet flavouring.
- Repeat with the remaining gelatine and sweetner and the strawberry flavouring.
- Gently fold the egg whites, little by little, into each mixture.
- Transfer both mixtures to small rectangular moulds (preferably silicone) and leave to set in the fridge for 1 hour. To serve, cut into bite-sized cubes.

Truffles

2 servings | Preparation time: 15 minutes
Refrigeration time: 4 hours

PP - PV

---

4 teaspoons sugar-free fat-reduced cocoa powder,
plus extra for dusting
1 tablespoon virtually fat-free quark
2 egg yolks
5 drops melted butter flavouring
3 tablespoons Canderel granules
5 tablespoons powdered skimmed milk

- Mix the cocoa powder into the quark until you get a thick creamy texture.

- Add the egg yolks, butter flavouring and sweetener and stir thoroughly. Add the powdered skimmed milk, tablespoon by tablespoon, so that the mixture becomes hard. If you are having difficulty mixing the ingredients properly, add a spoonful of water to create a paste. If, on the other hand, your mixture is too runny, add a little extra powdered skimmed milk.

- Using small spoons, shape the paste into little balls and arrange them on a plate covered with some greaseproof paper. Leave the truffles to rest in the fridge for at least 4 hours.

- Roll the truffles in some cocoa powder sprinkled on to a plate to dust them lightly before serving.

Dukan Pistachio Loukoumi

2 servings | Preparation time: 10 minutes
Resting time: overnight

PP - PV

---

1 rounded teaspoon agar-agar
2 teaspoons liquid Hermesetas
200ml (7fl oz) water
50ml (2fl oz) rose water
½ teaspoon pistachio flavouring
Cornflour and Canderel granules, for dusting

- In a saucepan, combine the agar-agar with the liquid sweetener, water, rose water and pistachio flavouring. Bring to the boil, simmer for a few minutes and then switch off the heat.

- Pour the mixture into small rectangular finger-biscuit-type silicone moulds. Leave to cool.

- When it has cooled, turn the loukoumi out on to a work top dusted with cornflour. Cut into cubes and leave on a plate, covered with a clean tea towel, to dry overnight.

- The following day, put a mixture of cornflour and Canderel granules in a small plastic container and add the loukoumi cubes. Close the container securely and shake to coat the cubes. Enjoy the loukoumi quickly before they become moist.

Banana Marshmallows

4 servings | Preparation time: 15 minutes
Refrigeration time: 2 hours | Resting time: 24 hours

PP - PV

800ml (28fl oz) water
4 tablespoons Splenda granules
3 egg whites
Pinch of salt
1½ × 2g sachets agar-agar
½ teaspoon banana flavouring
Canderel granules, for dusting

- Heat the water in a pan and add the sweetener.
- Meanwhile, beat the egg whites with the salt in a bowl until very stiff.
- Add the agar-agar and banana flavouring to the water, then remove the pan from the heat.
- Whisk up the egg whites again and pour in the banana water, stirring continuously. The mixture should keep increasing in volume. Stop beating when it becomes lukewarm.
- Pour the mixture into small rectangular finger-biscuit-type silicone moulds or use a piping bag to shape into strips on a baking tray. Put in the fridge to set for 2 hours, then take out and leave to dry for 24 hours.
- When the mixture is quite dry, cut into cubes. Put some Canderel granules in a plastic container, add the cubes, close and shake to coat the marshmallows. Remove the marshmallow cubes and shake them in a sieve to remove any excess sweetener.

Chocolate and Mandarin Cereal Bars

4 servings | Preparation time: 15 minutes
Freezing time: 1½ hours minimum

PP - PV

---

8 tablespoons oat bran
7 tablespoons powdered skimmed milk
6 tablespoons Canderel granules
3 tablespoons water
2 teaspoons mandarin flavouring
4 teaspoons sugar-free fat-reduced cocoa powder
1 tablespoon fat-free fromage frais

- In a small bowl, combine the oat bran with 4 tablespoons of the powdered skimmed milk, 3 tablespoons of the sweetener, 2 tablespoons of the water and the mandarin flavouring. Mix together so that you get a smooth, compact paste.

- Line a rectangular plastic container with clingfilm. Spread the oat mixture evenly over the bottom and freeze for at least half an hour.

- In another bowl, combine the cocoa powder with the remaining 3 tablespoons powdered milk and 3 tablespoons sweetener and the fromage frais. If necessary, add the remaining tablespoon of water to get a semi-liquid cream.

- Pour this cream over the oat bran and return to the freezer for at least 1 hour to become hard.

- Turn out of the container and cut into four bars. Store the bars in the fridge.

Violet and Blackcurrant Bonbons

4 servings | Preparation time: 5 minutes
Refrigeration time: 3 hours minimum

PP - PV

200ml (7fl oz) water (preferably mineral)
1 × 2g sachet agar-agar
10 drops violet flavouring
2 tablespoons Splenda granules, plus extra for dusting
10 drops food colouring (optional)
10 drops blackcurrant flavouring

- Bring half the water to the boil in a small saucepan.
- Dissolve half the agar-agar in the boiling water and add the violet flavouring, 1 tablespoon of the sweetener and food colouring (if using). Leave to simmer for 1 minute.
- Pour the mixture into a silicone ice-cube tray and leave to cool in the fridge for at least 3 hours.
- Repeat the process with the remaining water, agar-agar and sweetner, and the blackcurrant flavouring, again adding your choice of food colouring if you wish.
- Turn the cubes out and if necessary dust with sweetener to taste.
- These bonbons can be made with any food flavouring of your choice, as well as with diet cola.

Belle-Hélène Mousse with Silken Tofu

4 servings | **Preparation time: 15 minutes**
Refrigeration time: 3 hours minimum

PP - PV

---

4 gelatine leaves
300g (10½oz) silken tofu
200g (7oz) virtually fat-free quark
2 teaspoons pear flavouring
4 teaspoons sugar-free fat-reduced cocoa powder,
plus extra for dusting (optional)
500ml (18fl oz) skimmed milk
6 Canderel vanilla sticks

- Soak the gelatine leaves in a bowl of cold water.

- In a blender, combine the silken tofu, quark, pear flavouring, cocoa powder and about 400ml (14fl oz) of the milk. Blend until you get a frothy mixture.

- Heat the remaining milk in a small saucepan. Wring out the gelatine leaves and dissolve them in the hot milk. Add to the blender along with the vanilla sticks. Blend again.

- Pour the mixture into four glass sundae dishes and refrigerate for at least 3 hours. Dust with a little cocoa powder before serving, if you wish.

Zesty Lemon Mousse

4 servings | **Preparation time: 20 minutes**
Refrigeration time: 2 hours minimum

PP - PV

---

2 gelatine leaves
1 egg, separated
4 tablespoons Canderel granules
Grated zest of ½ unwaxed lemon
250g (9oz) fat-free fromage frais
1 teaspoon lemon flavouring
Pinch of salt

■ Soak the gelatine leaves in a bowl of cold water.

■ In another bowl, whisk together the egg yolk, 2 tablespoons of the sweetener, the grated lemon zest and 50g (1¾oz) of the fromage frais until the mixture is nice and smooth.

■ Transfer the mixture to a small saucepan and warm over a low heat for 2 minutes. Remove the pan from the heat. Carefully drain and wring the gelatine and add to the pan along with the lemon flavouring. Stir until all the ingredients have completely dissolved.

■ Whip the rest of the fromage frais and add to the lemon cream.

■ Beat the egg white with the salt until stiff. Then add the remaining 2 tablespoons sweetener and keep beating for a few more minutes.

■ Gently fold the beaten egg white into the lemon cream.

■ Pour into four glass dishes and refrigerate for at least 2 hours.

Whipped Marron Glacé Mousse

4 servings | **Preparation time: 15 minutes**
Refrigeration time: 2 hours minimum

PP - PV

---

4 eggs, separated
Pinch of salt
200g (7oz) silken tofu
2 teaspoons marron glacé flavouring
6 Canderel vanilla sticks

- In a bowl, beat the egg whites with the salt until very stiff.

- In another bowl, combine the silken tofu, egg yolks, marron glacé flavouring and vanilla sticks until the mixture is as smooth as possible.

- Gently fold the egg whites into the tofu mixture to produce a light marron glacé mousse. Pour it into four glass sundae dishes and refrigerate for at least 2 hours.

Mocha Mousse

4 servings | **Preparation time: 15 minutes**
Refrigeration time: 4 hours minimum

PP - PV

---

4 eggs, separated
Pinch of salt
4 teaspoons crystallized stevia
4 tablespoons 3% fat crème fraîche
30g (1oz) fat-free fromage frais
30g (1oz) virtually fat-free quark
1 tablespoon instant coffee granules
4 tablespoons sugar-free fat-reduced cocoa powder

- In a bowl, beat the egg whites with the salt until very stiff.

- In a saucepan, stir together the egg yolks and sweetener. Add the crème fraîche and warm over a low heat without allowing to boil.

- Once the cream has thickened, divide it between two bowls. To one bowl add the fromage frais and quark along with the instant coffee, and stir thoroughly. Add the cocoa powder to the second bowl and stir. Gently fold half the beaten egg whites into the mixture in each bowl. Check that both are sufficiently sweet and adjust if necessary.

- Pour a layer of the coffee mousse in four glass sundae dishes and top with a layer of the cocoa mousse. Refrigerate for at least 4 hours.

Minty Chocolate Mousse

4 servings | **Preparation time: 20 minutes**
Refrigeration time: 2 hours minimum

PP - PV

---

4 eggs, separated
8 tablespoons fat-free fromage frais
4 teaspoons sugar-free fat-reduced cocoa powder
4 tablespoons powdered skimmed milk
1 teaspoon peppermint flavouring
4 teaspoons crystallized stevia
Pinch of salt
4 fresh mint leaves

- In a bowl, mix together the egg yolks, fromage frais, cocoa powder, powdered skimmed milk, peppermint flavouring and sweetener.
- In another bowl, beat the egg whites with the salt until stiff. Gently fold into the choco-mint mixture.
- Pour the mixture into four glass dishes and refrigerate for at least 2 hours. Before serving, decorate each one with a fresh mint leaf.

Egg Custard

4 servings | **Preparation time: 15 minutes**
Cooking time: 30 minutes

PP - PV

---

6 eggs
500ml (18fl oz) skimmed milk
1 vanilla pod or 2 teaspoons vanilla flavouring
Pinch of grated nutmeg
6 Canderel vanilla sticks

- Preheat the oven to 160°C/325°F/Gas 3.
- Break the eggs into a bowl and whisk.
- Warm the milk in a saucepan with the vanilla pod (or flavouring) and nutmeg. Do not allow it to boil.
- Remove the vanilla pod before carefully pouring the milk over the eggs and adding the vanilla sticks.
- Pour the mixture into ramekin dishes and bake in a bain-marie in the preheated oven for 30 minutes, keeping a careful eye on them after about 20 minutes to check if they are ready.

Crème Caramel with Agar-Agar

4 servings | **Preparation time: 10 minutes**
Cooking time: 5 minutes | **Refrigeration time: 3 hours minimum**

PP - PV

---

1 litre (1¾ pints) skimmed milk
2 teaspoons agar-agar
1 teaspoon caramel flavouring
8 tablespoons Canderel granules

- Bring the milk to the boil in a saucepan.
- Turn the heat right down, add the agar-agar and stir thoroughly.
- Turn the heat off and add the caramel flavouring and sweetener.
- Pour the mixture into four individual dishes and leave to cool to room temperature before refrigerating for at least 3 hours.

Vanilla Crème Brûlée

4 servings | **Preparation time: 15 minutes**
Cooking time: 25 minutes

PP - PV

---

5 eggs
375ml (13fl oz) skimmed milk
1 vanilla pod
½ teaspoon crème brûlée flavouring
4 tablespoons Splenda granules
Pinch of grated nutmeg

- Preheat the oven to 160°C/325°F/Gas 3.

- Whisk the eggs together in a large bowl.

- Heat the milk in a saucepan with the vanilla pod and crème brûlée flavouring. Do not let it come to the boil.

- Remove the vanilla pod before carefully pouring the hot milk over the eggs and adding the sweetener and nutmeg.

- Pour the mixture into shallow ramekin dishes and bake in a bain-marie in the preheated oven for 20 minutes, until the cream is quite set. Remove from the oven, leave to cool a little and serve warm.

Fruit Jelly

4 servings | **Preparation time: 10 minutes**
Refrigeration time: overnight

PP - PV

600ml (20fl oz) water
8 gelatine leaves
30 drops fruit flavouring of your choice (e.g. blackcurrant,
lemon, orange, clementine, strawberry, raspberry,
passion fruit)
4–6 tablespoons Canderel granules
(depending on flavouring used)

- Bring the water to the boil in a saucepan. In the meantime, soak the gelatine leaves in a bowl of cold water.

- Once the water is boiling, turn the heat down and add the flavouring of your choice together with the drained softened gelatine leaves and sweetener. Stir all the ingredients together thoroughly and check the sweetness. Pour the jelly into a glass dish or dishes, or into small individual fluted moulds.

- Leave to cool to room temperature before refrigerating overnight.

Egg Cream

4 servings | **Preparation time: 15 minutes**
Cooking time: 20 minutes

PP - PV

500ml (18fl oz) skimmed milk
4 tablespoons Splenda granules
2 eggs + 2 egg yolks
1 Canderel vanilla stick

- Preheat the oven to 180°C/350°F/Gas 4.
- Pour the milk into a saucepan, bring to a simmer over a medium heat and then add the sweetener.
- In a bowl, mix together the eggs, egg yolks and vanilla stick.
- Pour the hot milk gently over the egg mixture and stir thoroughly. Pour into ramekin dishes and bake in the preheated oven for 20 minutes.
- Serve the creams in their ramekins, either hot straight from the oven or chilled.

Choc'Orangette Cream

4 servings | **Preparation time: 15 minutes**
Cooking time: 20 minutes

PP - PV

400ml (14fl oz) skimmed milk
4 pinches of ground cinnamon
4 teaspoons sugar-free fat-reduced cocoa powder,
plus extra for sprinkling
1 teaspoon orange flavouring
4 tablespoons Splenda granules
4 eggs

- Preheat the oven to 180°C/350°F/Gas 4.
- Bring the milk to the boil in a saucepan with the cinnamon. Add the cocoa powder, orange flavouring and sweetener, then leave to cool partially.
- In a bowl, beat the eggs, then gently fold them into the warm milk.
- Pour the mixture into ramekin dishes and bake in a bain-marie in the preheated oven for 20 minutes.
- Serve the creams either warm from the oven or chilled, with a little cocoa powder sprinkled on top.

Coffee Cream

4 servings | **Preparation time: 15 minutes**
Cooking time: 20 minutes

PP - PV

600ml (20fl oz) skimmed milk
1 teaspoon coffee essence (or instant coffee granules)
3 eggs
4 tablespoons Canderel granules

- Preheat the oven to 180°C/350°F/Gas 4.
- Bring the milk to the boil in a saucepan with the coffee essence.
- In a bowl, beat the eggs with the sweetener and gently add to the milk, stirring continuously.
- Pour the mixture into ramekin dishes and bake in a bain-marie in the preheated oven for 20 minutes.
- Serve chilled.

Orange-flavoured Earl Grey Cream

4 servings | **Preparation time: 15 minutes**
Cooking time: 20 minutes

PP - PV

---

4 eggs
4 tablespoons Canderel granules
250ml (9fl oz) skimmed milk
250ml (9fl oz) Earl Grey tea (or very strong orange-flavoured tea)
Grated zest of 2 unwaxed oranges
1 teaspoon orange flavouring

- Preheat the oven to 160°C/325°F/Gas 3.

- In a saucepan, mix together the eggs, sweetener, milk, tea, half the orange zest and the orange flavouring. Warm over a gentle heat for a few moments, stirring all the time.

- Pour this mixture into four ramekin dishes and bake in a bain-marie in the preheated oven for 20 minutes.

- Remove from the oven and leave to cool for 30 minutes. Serve decorated with the remaining orange zest.

Vanilla Custard Flan

4 servings | **Preparation time: 10 minutes**
Cooking time: 50 minutes

PP - PV

500ml (18fl oz) skimmed milk
2 tablespoons vanilla flavouring or 1 vanilla pod
2 eggs
6 Canderel vanilla sticks
4 tablespoons cornflour

- Preheat the oven to 180°C/350°F/Gas 4.

- Warm the milk in a saucepan with the vanilla flavouring (or vanilla pod).

- Break the eggs into a bowl and beat well. Add the vanilla sticks, then the cornflour, and mix together thoroughly. Pour in the hot milk (first remove the vanilla pod, if using), stirring continuously. Return the mixture to the pan and continue stirring for a few minutes over a gentle heat until it starts to thicken.

- Pour the mixture into a non-stick 21cm (8in) tin and bake in the preheated oven for 40 minutes. When the flan is cooked, place it under a hot grill for a few seconds to brown the top.

Panna Cotta with Passion Fruit Jelly

4 servings | **Preparation time: 25 minutes**
Refrigeration time: 3 hours minimum + overnight

PP - PV

---

6 gelatine leaves
150ml (5fl oz) water
1 teaspoon liquid Hermesetas
1 teaspoon passion fruit flavouring
500ml (18fl oz) skimmed milk
2 teaspoons vanilla flavouring
500ml (18fl oz) 3% fat single cream
4 tablespoons Canderel granules

- Soak 2 of the gelatine leaves in a bowl of cold water.

- Heat the measured water in a saucepan with the liquid sweetener. Wring dry the gelatine leaves and add to the pan along with the passion fruit flavouring.

- Pour into the bottom of four glass sundae or stemmed dishes. Refrigerate until the gelatine has set (at least 3 hours). Once the jelly is ready, make the panna cotta.

- Soak the remaining 4 gelatine leaves in a bowl of cold water. Pour the milk into a saucepan and add the vanilla flavouring. Warm over a gentle heat and then add the cream. Drain the gelatine leaves and dissolve in the hot milk in the pan.

- Remove the pan from the heat and stir in the granulated sweetener. Cool the panna cotta mixture a little before very carefully pouring it into the dishes, so as not to melt the jelly underneath. Refrigerate overnight.

Istanbul Muhallebi

4 servings | **Preparation time: 5 minutes**
Cooking time: 12 minutes | **Refrigeration time: 4 hours minimum**

PP - PV

---

4 tablespoons cornflour
600ml (20fl oz) skimmed milk
4 tablespoons Canderel granules
2 tablespoons orange flower water (or rose water)
Ground cinnamon, for dusting

- In a bowl, gradually mix the cornflour with a little of the milk until you get a smooth paste.

- Pour the rest of the milk into a saucepan and warm over a medium heat. As soon as the milk begins to simmer, add the cornflour paste and whisk vigorously. Still over a medium heat, bring to the boil, whisking continuously, then turn the heat down and continue beating until the mixture is thick enough to coat the back of a spoon. Add the sweetener and orange flower water, stir well and remove from the heat.

- Pour the mixture into four ramekin dishes and refrigerate for at least 4 hours. Just before you are ready to serve, sprinkle some ground cinnamon over the top.

Blueberry Delight

4 servings | **Preparation time: 15 minutes**
Refrigeration time: 3 hours minimum

PP - PV

---

4 gelatine leaves
75ml (2½fl oz) water
600g (1lb 5oz) fat-free blueberry yoghurt
For the Dukan Chantilly:
2 teaspoons crystallized stevia
4 tablespoons fat-free cottage cheese,
drained for at least ½ day
4 egg whites
Pinch of salt

- Soak the gelatine in a bowl of cold water until completely softened.

- Bring the water to the boil in a small saucepan. Add the drained gelatine and stir to dissolve.

- Turn the yoghurt into a bowl and add the gelatine water. Pour into four sundae dishes and refrigerate for at least 3 hours.

- To make the Dukan Chantilly, stir the sweetener into the drained cottage cheese. Beat the egg whites with the salt until very stiff.

- Fold the beaten egg whites very carefully into the cottage cheese and refrigerate.

- When ready to serve, add a little Dukan Chantilly to each dish of blueberry delight.

Morello Cherry and Almond Panna Cotta

4 servings | **Preparation time: 15 minutes**
Refrigeration time: 4 hours minimum

PP - PV

---

4 gelatine leaves
400g (14oz) silken tofu
1 teaspoon morello cherry flavouring
4 teaspoons crystallized stevia
1 teaspoon bitter almond flavouring
4 tablespoons skimmed milk

- Soften the gelatine in a shallow bowl of cold water.

- Put half of the tofu in a blender. Add the morello cherry flavouring and half the sweetener. Blend until the mixture is nice and smooth.

- Fill the bottom half of four glass sundae dishes with this mixture.

- Start the process again with the rest of the tofu, the almond flavouring and the remaining sweetener.

- Warm the milk in a small saucepan over a gentle heat. Drain the gelatine and add to the hot milk. Once the gelatine has fully dissolved, stir the milk gently but quickly into the bitter almond and tofu mixture. Blend until very smooth and then fill the upper part of the sundae dishes. Refrigerate for at least 4 hours.

Chocobanana Cream with Silken Tofu

4 servings | **Preparation time: 10 minutes**
Refrigeration time: 6 hours

PP - PV

300g (10½oz) silken tofu
500ml (18fl oz) skimmed milk
1 teaspoon banana flavouring
4 teaspoons sugar-free fat-reduced cocoa powder
6 Canderel vanilla sticks
300g (10½oz) fat-free vanilla yoghurt (e.g. Sveltesse)

■ Put all the ingredients into a blender and blend until the mixture is nice and creamy.

■ Pour the cream into four large glasses and place in the fridge for 6 hours. Stir before serving.

Chocolate Log

**6 servings | Preparation time: 30 minutes | Cooking time: 15 minutes
Refrigeration time: 2 hours minimum**

PP - PV

For the cream filling:
300ml (10fl oz) skimmed milk
4 gelatine leaves
2 eggs
2 tablespoons cornflour
4 tablespoons Splenda granules
2 teaspoons dark chocolate flavouring
For the sponge:
6 eggs, separated
1 × 7g sachet dried yeast
4 tablespoons cornflour

150g (5½oz) Splenda granules
2 teaspoons orange flower water
2 teaspoons vanilla flavouring
Pinch of salt
For the icing:
4 teaspoons sugar-free reduced-fat
cocoa powder, plus extra for dusting
3 tablespoons Splenda granules
7 tablespoons powdered
skimmed milk
75ml (2½fl oz) skimmed milk

■ To make the cream filling, heat the milk in a saucepan over a low heat. Soak the gelatine leaves in a dish of cold water. In a bowl, mix the eggs with the cornflour, sweetener and dark chocolate flavouring. Stir together thoroughly to get a smooth paste. Gradually add the hot milk, stirring continuously. Return the mixture to the pan and heat, stirring all the while, until it starts to thicken. Add the well-drained gelatine leaves and stir again to dissolve, then refrigerate the cream.

■ In the meantime, prepare the sponge. Preheat the oven to 180°C/350°F/Gas 4 and line a 33 x 22cm (12 x 8in) baking tin with greaseproof paper. Combine the egg yolks with the yeast, cornflour, sweetener, orange flower water and vanilla flavouring. In a separate bowl, beat the egg whites with the salt until stiff. Gently fold them into the egg yolk mixture and spread over the baking sheet to a thickness of about 1cm (½in) in a good rectangular shape that you will be able to roll up into a log. Bake in the middle of the preheated oven for 8–10 minutes. Allow to cool slightly. Taking care that it does not break up, transfer the sponge to a damp clean tea towel so that it is easier to roll up. Spread the cream over the top of the sponge and roll it up lengthways.

■ To make the icing, mix the cocoa powder with the sweetener and skimmed milk powder. Add the milk gradually to ensure that the icing is thick but spreadable and then cover the log. Sprinkle over some cocoa powder and refrigerate for at least 2 hours.

Mocha Mousse Log

**4 servings | Preparation time: 30 minutes | Cooking time: 15 minutes
Refrigeration time: 2 hours minimum**

PP - PV

For the mocha mousse:
1 small cup very strong espresso
coffee
2 × 2g sachets agar-agar
30g (1oz) fat-free fromage frais
30g (1oz) virtually fat-free quark
1 egg, separated
4 tablespoons Canderel granules
1 teaspoon mocha flavouring
Pinch of salt
For the sponge:
3 eggs, separated
1 teaspoon dried yeast
1 teaspoon liquid Hermesetas

2 tablespoons Protifar powder
2 tablespoons powdered
skimmed milk
2 tablespoons skimmed milk
1 teaspoon vanilla flavouring
Pinch of salt
For the mocha cream:
100ml (3½fl oz) skimmed milk
1 teaspoon agar-agar
60g (2¼oz) fat-free fromage frais
60g (2¼oz) virtually
fat-free quark
4 tablespoons Canderel granules
1 teaspoon mocha flavouring

- First make the mocha mousse. Heat the espresso in a saucepan with the agar-agar. Boil for 1 minute. In a bowl, combine the fromage frais and quark with the egg yolk, sweetener and mocha flavouring. In a separate bowl, beat the egg white with the salt until very stiff. Combine all the ingredients and then refrigerate the mousse.

- In the meantime, prepare the sponge. Preheat the oven to180°C/350°F/ Gas 4 and line a 33 x 22cm (12 x 8in) baking tin with greaseproof paper. Mix the egg yolks with the yeast, liquid sweetener, protein powder, powdered milk, skimmed milk and vanilla flavouring. In a separate bowl, beat the egg whites with the salt until very stiff. Gently fold them into the egg yolk mixture and spread over the baking sheet to a thickness of about 1cm (½in) in a good rectangular shape that you will be able to roll up into a log. Bake in the middle of the preheated oven for 8–10 minutes – be careful not to overcook. Allow to cool slightly. Transfer the sponge to a damp tea towel so that it is easier to roll up. Spread the cream over the top of the sponge and roll it up lengthways.

- To make the mocha cream, bring the skimmed milk to the boil in a saucepan and add the agar-agar. In a bowl, stir together the fromage frais, quark, sweetener and mocha flavouring. Add the milk. Cover the log with the mocha cream and refrigerate for at least 2 hours.

Cream Puffs

4 servings | Preparation time: 30 minutes
Cooking time: 20 minutes

PP - PV

For the choux pastry:
4 eggs, separated
Pinch of salt
2 tablespoons cornflour
2 tablespoons Splenda granules, plus extra for dusting
30g (1oz) fat-free fromage frais
30g (1oz) virtually fat-free quark
2 teaspoons vanilla flavouring
2 teaspoons dried yeast
For the vanilla crème pâtissière:
500ml (18fl oz) skimmed milk
2 teaspoons vanilla flavouring
4 egg yolks
2 tablespoons cornflour
2 tablespoons Splenda granules

■ Preheat the oven to 180°C/350°F/Gas 4. To make the choux pastry, beat the egg whites with the salt until very stiff. In another bowl, stir together the egg yolks, cornflour, sweetener, fromage frais, quark, vanilla flavouring and yeast. Mix until nice and smooth. Very carefully fold the beaten egg whites into this mixture and pour into mini-muffin or petit-four tins. Increase the oven temperature to 200°C/400°F/Gas 6 and bake for 15 minutes, keeping a careful eye on the puffs to check when they are ready.

■ Meanwhile, make the vanilla crème pâtissière. Warm 450ml (16fl oz) of the milk with the vanilla flavouring over a low heat. In a bowl, combine the remaining milk with the egg yolks, cornflour and sweetener. Pour the egg mixture into the hot milk, stirring continuously until the cream starts to thicken. Remove the pan from the heat and continue stirring for a few minutes. Leave the choux puffs and the crème pâtissière to cool. When they are cool, cut off the tops of the puffs and hollow them out carefully. Using a piping bag, fill the insides with the cream and then put the tops back on. Chill in the fridge before serving.

Millefeuilles

4 servings | Preparation time: 30 minutes | Cooking time: 30 minutes
Refrigeration time: 1 hour minimum

PP - PV

For the pastry and icing:
4 eggs, separated + 4 egg yolks
1 teaspoon melted butter flavouring
2 tablespoons cornflour
1 tablespoon Splenda granules
For the crème pâtissière:
4 gelatine leaves
2 eggs
2 level teaspoons cornflour
4 tablespoons Splenda granules
2 teaspoons vanilla flavouring

■ Preheat the oven to 180°C/350°F/Gas 4 and line a baking sheet with greaseproof paper. To make the pastry, mix together the egg yolks with the butter flavouring and cornflour. Beat 3 of the egg whites until very stiff and gently fold them into the mixture. Pour on to the baking sheet to form thin circles of the same diameter. Bake in the preheated oven for 20 minutes, checking regularly.

■ Meanwhile, make the crème pâtissière. Soak the gelatine leaves in some cold water. Mix the eggs in a bowl with the cornflour, sweetener and vanilla flavouring, and stir together until you get a very smooth cream. Heat the milk in a small saucepan. Add the hot milk to the eggs and stir. Return to the pan and warm the cream over a low heat, stirring until it thickens. Remove the pan from the heat. Drain and wring the gelatine leaves and add them to the cream, stirring to dissolve completely. Leave to cool.

■ To make the icing, beat the remaining egg white until stiff and add the sweetener.

■ To assemble the millefeuilles, take one baked pastry circle and spread some cream over it, cover with another pastry circle and cream then repeat this process until only one pastry circle is left. Place this on top, spread with the icing and leave to set in the fridge for at least 1 hour.

Chocolate Fondant

4 servings | Preparation time: 10 minutes
Cooking time: 6–12 minutes, depending on the oven

PP - PV

---

3 eggs
3 tablespoons cornflour
3 tablespoons fat-free fromage frais
3 tablespoons virtually fat-free quark
3 teaspoons sugar-free reduced-fat cocoa powder
1½ tablespoons liquid Hermesetas
1 teaspoon baking powder

- Using an electric whisk, combine all the ingredients and pour the mixture into a small microwavable dish. Cover with either a lid or some clingfilm.

- Microwave on maximum power for 6 minutes. Alternatively, bake, uncovered, in a preheated conventional oven at 180°C/350°F/Gas 4 for 10–12 minutes.

- When the fondant is cooked, remove the dish from the oven and place it on a sheet of kitchen paper to rest for a few minutes.

'The Residence' Tiramisù

**4 servings | Preparation time: 30 minutes | Cooking time: 10 minutes
Refrigeration time: 30 minutes minimum**

PP - PV

For the crème pâtissière:
400ml (14fl oz) skimmed milk, plus extra for mixing
½ vanilla pod
3 tablespoons cornflour
2 eggs + 1 egg yolk
4 tablespoons Splenda granules
40g (1½oz) fat-free fromage frais
For the sponge:
1 egg, separated
2½ level tablespoons

Splenda granules
1 teaspoon vanilla flavouring
Grated zest of ½ unwaxed lemon
1 tablespoon cornflour
¼ × 8g sachet baking powder
4 tablespoons coffee, to soak the sponge
Sugar-free fat-reduced cocoa powder, for sprinkling

■ To make the crème pâtissière, bring the milk to the boil in a saucepan with the vanilla pod. Dissolve the cornflour in a little cold milk. Whisk the eggs and yolk with the sweetener, add the cornflour mixture, then pour in a third of the boiling milk. Pour this mixture back into the remaining milk in the pan and heat, stirring continuously, until it starts to thicken. Stir the fromage frais into 200g (7oz) of the crème pâtissière (save the remainder for another dish).

■ Make the tiramisù sponge. Preheat the oven to 180°C/350°F/Gas 4 and line a baking sheet with greaseproof paper. In a bowl, whisk together the egg yolk with the sweetener and vanilla flavouring until the mixture is nice and creamy. Add the lemon zest, cornflour and baking powder. Beat the egg white until very stiff and fold it into the creamy mixture. Place on the baking sheet and bake in the preheated oven for 10 minutes or so. Transfer the sponge to a wire rack to cool. Using a pastry cutter the same size as your sundae dishes, cut the sponge into 12 small circles. Place one in each dish and soak with the coffee. Cover with a layer of crème pâtissière and sprinkle over a little cocoa powder. Repeat until you have three layers of sponge in each dish. Refrigerate for at least 30 minutes before serving.

■ Many thanks to The Residence Hotel in Tunis and Feker Jlassi, the pastry chef, for this delicious recipe.

Dukan Cannelés

4 servings | Preparation time: 10 minutes
Cooking time: 1 hour 5 minutes

PP - PV

250ml (9fl oz) skimmed milk
2 teaspoons vanilla flavouring
5 tablespoons cornflour
3 tablespoons Splenda granules
1 egg + 1 egg yolk
½ teaspoon rum flavouring

- Preheat the oven to 230°C/450°F/Gas 8.

- Bring the milk to the boil in a saucepan with the vanilla flavouring.

- In a bowl, stir together the cornflour, sweetener and eggs. Pour the boiling milk over the egg mixture, then add the rum flavouring. Stir gently until you get a runny mixture and then leave it to cool.

- Pour the mixture into silicone cannelé moulds (or small fluted moulds) and bake in the preheated oven for 5 minutes. Lower the oven temperature to 180°C/350°F/ Gas 4 and bake for a further 1 hour. The cannelés should have a nice brown crust but be soft and chewy inside.

Dukan Rum Babas

**4 servings | Preparation time: 20 minutes
Cooking time: 20 minutes**

PP - PV

For the babas:
4 eggs, separated
4 tablespoons Splenda granules
4 tablespoons oat bran
2 tablespoons wheat bran
2 tablespoons cornflour
1 × 8g sachet baking powder
160ml (5½fl oz) skimmed milk
Pinch of salt
For the rum syrup:
150ml (5fl oz) water
2 Canderel vanilla sticks
2 teaspoons rum flavouring
For the Dukan Chantilly:
60g (2¼oz) fat-free fromage frais
60g (2¼oz) virtually fat-free quark
1 teaspoon vanilla flavouring
4 Canderel vanilla sticks
2 egg whites

- Preheat the oven to 180°C/350°F/Gas 4.
- Stir together the egg yolks, sweetener, oat and wheat brans, cornflour, baking powder and skimmed milk. In a separate bowl, beat the egg whites with the salt until stiff. Gently fold the egg whites into the bran mixture and pour it into four small aluminium rum baba moulds. Bake in the preheated oven for 20 minutes.
- Meanwhile, prepare the rum syrup. Heat the water in a small pan with the vanilla sticks and rum flavouring. Once the babas are done, turn them out of the moulds and pour the syrup over them, letting it soak right in.
- To make the Dukan Chantilly, mix together the fromage frais, quark, vanilla flavouring and vanilla sticks. Beat the egg whites until very stiff and gently fold them into the mixture.
- Serve the rum babas topped with a little of the Dukan Chantilly.

Ultra-light Chocolate Sponge Cake

**2 servings | Preparation time: 10 minutes
Cooking time: 20 minutes**

PP - PV

---

4 eggs, separated
2 teaspoons sugar-free reduced-fat cocoa powder
5 tablespoons Splenda granules
Grated zest of 1 unwaxed orange
40g (1½oz) cornflour

- Preheat the oven to 180°C/350°F/Gas 4 and line a 18cm (7in) cake tin with greaseproof paper.
- In a bowl, beat the egg whites until stiff.
- In another bowl, stir together the egg yolks, cocoa powder and sweetener, then add the orange zest and cornflour. Gently fold in the beaten egg whites.
- Pour the mixture into the cake tin and bake in the preheated oven for 20 minutes, keeping a careful eye on the cake. When it is nicely coloured on top, it is ready.

Floating Islands

**4 servings | Preparation time: 15 minutes | Cooking time: 20 minutes
Refrigeration time: 2 hours minimum**

PP - PV

800ml (28fl oz) skimmed milk
2 teaspoons vanilla flavouring
4 eggs, separated
8 Canderel vanilla sticks
Pinch of salt

- Heat the milk and vanilla flavouring in a saucepan over a low heat. Beat the egg yolks, stir in the vanilla sticks and gently pour into the hot milk, stirring all the time with a wooden spoon. Continue to heat the milk over a gentle heat until it is thick enough to coat the back of the spoon.

- Fill another pan with water and bring to the boil.

- In a separate bowl, beat the egg whites with the salt until very stiff. Use the beaten egg whites to make quenelles, or small balls, and poach them on both sides in the pan of boiling water.

- Pour the custard cream into a large bowl and arrange the poached egg whites on top. Refrigerate for at least 2 hours before serving.

Dukan Whipped Chestnut Mousse

4 servings | Preparation time: 10 minutes
Refrigeration time: 2 hours minimum

PP - PV

120g (4¼oz) virtually fat-free quark
120g (4¼oz) fat-free fromage frais
4 tablespoons 3% fat crème fraîche
1 teaspoon marron glacé flavouring
4 teaspoons crystallized stevia
3 egg whites
Pinch of salt

- In a bowl, stir together the quark, fromage frais, low-fat crème fraîche, marron glacé flavouring and sweetener.

- In a separate bowl, beat the egg whites with the salt until very stiff. Fold into the fromage frais and quark mixture.

- Pour the mousse into individual sundae dishes and refrigerate for at least 2 hours. Serve well chilled.

Dukan Black Forest Gâteau

4 servings | Preparation time: 20 minutes
Cooking time: 20 minutes

PP - PV

For the jelly:
5 tablespoons sugar-free
strawberry-pomegranate or
raspberry-cranberry syrup
(e.g.Teisseire)
1 tablespoon Splenda granules
1 teaspoon morello
cherry flavouring
1 teaspoon agar-agar
For the Dukan Chantilly:
2 egg whites
Pinch of salt
2 Canderel vanilla sticks
30g (1oz) virtually fat-free quark
30g (1oz) fat-free fromage frais

For the gâteau:
4 tablespoons oat bran
2 tablespoons wheat bran
1 tablespoon cornflour
3 teaspoons sugar-free
reduced-fat cocoa powder
2 eggs
150g (5½oz) fat-free
natural yoghurt
5 tablespoons Splenda
granules
1 × 8g sachet baking powder
1 teaspoon dark chocolate
flavouring

- To make the jelly, heat the syrup, sweetener, morello cherry flavouring and agar-agar in a small saucepan. Bring to the boil and simmer for 1 minute. Take the pan off the heat, leave to cool, then place the jelly in the fridge to set.

- Next prepare the Dukan Chantilly. Beat the egg whites with the salt until very stiff. Add the vanilla sticks and continue beating. Put the quark and fromage frais in a bowl and carefully fold in the beaten egg whites.

- Preheat the oven to 180°C 350°F/Gas 4.

- In a bowl, combine all the ingredients for the gâteau. Pour the mixture into a 21cm (8in) round silicone cake mould and bake in the preheated oven for 20 minutes. Remove the gâteau from the oven and leave to cool. Then, using a thin, very sharp-bladed knife, cut it in two horizontally. Sandwich the two layers together with half the jelly and spread the rest on top. Fill a piping bag with the Dukan Chantilly and pipe the cream over the gâteau.

Dukan Coffee Eclairs

4 servings | Preparation time: 30 minutes | Cooking time: 20 minutes

PP - PV

For the eclairs:
2 eggs, separated
Pinch of salt
1 teaspoon liquid Hermesetas
1 tablespoon cornflour
1 teaspoon baking powder
1 teaspoon vanilla flavouring
For the cream filling:
60g (2¼oz) virtually fat-free quark
60g (2¼oz) fat-free fromage frais
4 tablespoons
Canderel granules

2 teaspoons instant coffee granules
125ml (4fl oz) skimmed milk
1 × 2g sachet agar-agar
For the icing:
1 egg white
8 tablespoons
Canderel granules
1 teaspoon
coffee flavouring
3 tablespoons
powdered skimmed milk

- Preheat the oven to 180°C/350°F/Gas 4.

- To make the eclairs, beat the egg whites with the salt until very stiff. In another bowl, stir together the egg yolks, liquid sweetener, cornflour, baking powder and vanilla flavouring. Gently fold in the beaten egg whites, then use this mixture to form four long (or eight small) eclair shapes on a baking sheet. Bake in the preheated oven for 15 minutes, keeping a careful eye on the eclairs to check when they are ready. Remove from the oven and leave them to cool a little. Use a sharp-bladed knife to remove the upper half of each eclair.

- Meanwhile, prepare the cream filling. In a large bowl, combine the quark, fromage frais, sweetener and instant coffee. In a small saucepan, heat the milk and add the agar-agar. Bring to the boil, then remove from the heat and stir the milk into the quark and fromage frais mixture. Use this cream to fill the bottom half of the eclairs and then put the tops back on.

- In a separate bowl, stir together the egg white and sweetener to make the icing. Add the coffee flavouring. Blend the powdered milk as finely as possible and gradually sprinkle it into the mixture. The icing should be fairly thick. Spread it over each eclair, then refrigerate to chill the eclairs and to harden the icing.

Choco-raspberry and Choco-mint Cupcakes

4 servings | Preparation time: 30 minutes | Cooking time: 15 minutes

PP - PV

---

4 tablespoons oat bran
2 tablespoons wheat bran
4 teaspoons sugar-free reduced-fat cocoa powder
2 teaspoons liquid Hermesetas
1 × 8g sachet baking powder
2 tablespoons fat-free fromage frais
4 eggs
10 teaspoons Canderel granules
6 drops red-pink food colouring
½ teaspoon raspberry flavouring
6 drops green food colouring
½ teaspoon peppermint flavouring
4 tablespoons powdered skimmed milk

- Preheat the oven to 180°C/350°F/Gas 4.

- In a bowl, stir together the oat and wheat brans, cocoa powder and liquid sweetener. Next add the baking powder and fromage frais. Break 2 of the eggs into a bowl and separate the whites from the yolks. Add the yolks to the bran mixture along with the remaining 2 whole eggs. Put the 2 egg whites to one side. Pour the bran mixture into silicone muffin moulds and bake in the preheated oven for 15 minutes, keeping a careful eye on the cupcakes to check when they are ready.

- In the meantime, make the icing. Add the granulated sweetener to the reserved egg whites. Divide the egg whites between two bowls. To one bowl add the red-pink food colouring and raspberry flavouring and to the other the green food colouring and peppermint flavouring. Finely blend the powdered milk and sprinkle carefully into both bowls, stirring gradually until you get the nice thick texture of traditional icing. Ice half the cupcakes with the raspberry icing and the other half with the peppermint icing. Refrigerate so that the icing hardens.

Dukan Galette des Rois (Twelfth Night Cake)

4 servings | Preparation time: 20 minutes | Cooking time: 27 minutes

PP - PV

For the frangipane-style filling:
2 eggs
1 tablespoon wheat bran
2 tablespoons oat bran
3 tablespoons Canderel granules
2 tablespoons fat-free fromage frais
4 tablespoons protein powder (such as Protifar)
2 teaspoons bitter almond flavouring
For the galette:
3 eggs, separated
Pinch of salt
½ × 8g sachet baking powder
4 tablespoons protein powder (such as Protifar)
75ml (2½fl oz) skimmed milk
4 tablespoons Canderel granules
1 teaspoon hazelnut flavouring

- Preheat the oven to 180°C/350°F/Gas 4.

- In a bowl, mix together all the ingredients for the frangipane filling and put to one side.

- To make the galette, beat the egg whites with the salt until very stiff. In a separate bowl, stir the rest of the ingredients together and gently fold in the beaten egg whites. Spread the mixture evenly into two round 18cm (7in) silicone cake moulds, or tins lined with greaseproof paper, and bake in the preheated oven for 6–7 minutes.

- Remove the galettes from the moulds and sandwich the frangipane filling between the two. Place on a baking sheet and return the whole cake to the oven for a further 20 minutes.

- Traditionally, a lucky charm, or *fève*, might be hidden in the filling – a bit like the British custom of inserting a sixpence in the Christmas pudding.

Dukan St Tropez Cake

4 servings | Preparation time: 20 minutes
Rising time: 2 hours minimum | Cooking time: 30 minutes

PP - PV

For the cream filling:
500ml (18fl oz) skimmed milk
1 tablespoon
vanilla flavouring
1 vanilla pod
2 egg yolks
2 tablespoons Splenda granules
2 tablespoons cornflour
1 tablespoon orange flower
water
For the cake:*
4 tablespoons oat bran

2 tablespoons wheat bran
2 eggs
2 tablespoons Splenda granules,
plus extra for dusting
4 tablespoons powdered
skimmed milk
150g (5½oz) sugar-free, fat-free
vanilla yoghurt (e.g. Sveltesse)
15g (½oz) dried yeast dissolved
in 1 tablespoon skimmed milk
2 tablespoons orange
flower water

- To make the cream filling, pour the skimmed milk into a saucepan. Add the vanilla flavouring and the vanilla pod, split in half, and bring to the boil. Mix the egg yolks with the sweetener, then add the cornflour and orange flower water. As soon as the milk reaches boiling point, pour the egg mixture into the pan and stir with a wooden spoon until the cream starts to thicken and coats the back of the spoon. Remove from the heat and leave to cool.

- Blend the oat and wheat brans to break them down further. In a bowl, whisk the eggs with the sweetener. Add the brans and all the remaining cake ingredients. Knead together, then cover with a tea towel and leave the dough to swell for at least 2 hours in a warm place.

- Preheat the oven to 180°C/350°F/Gas 4 and line a 18cm (7in) flan dish with greaseproof paper. Spread the dough evenly to fill the flan dish and bake in the preheated oven for about 25 minutes. Once the cake is ready, leave it to cool down. When it is quite cold, cut it in two horizontally and sandwich the cream (remove the vanilla pod) between the two halves. Sprinkle over a little extra sweetener and chill in the fridge before serving.

*It is also possible to make this cake using a light sponge (see page 60).

Dukan Fiadone (Corsican Cheesecake)

**4 servings | Preparation time: 15 minutes
Cooking time: 45 minutes**

PP - PV

---

6 eggs, separated
600g (1lb 5oz) virtually fat-free cottage cheese, well drained
6 tablespoons Splenda granules
2 teaspoons lemon flavouring
Grated zest of 1 unwaxed lemon
Pinch of salt

- Preheat the oven to 180°C/350°F/Gas 4.
- In a bowl, beat the egg whites with the salt until very stiff.
- In another, large bowl, stir the egg yolks into the cottage cheese. Add the sweetener, lemon flavouring and lemon zest. Gently fold in the beaten egg whites.
- Pour the mixture into a 18cm (7in) high-sided silicone flan dish and bake in the preheated oven for about 45 minutes, keeping a careful eye on the cheesecake to check when it is ready.

Pain Perdu

4 servings | Preparation time: 20 minutes
Cooking time: 10 minutes

PP - PV

For the bread:
4 tablespoons oat bran
1 × 8g sachet baking powder
2 tablespoons fat-free fromage frais
2 eggs
For the eggy dip:
2 eggs
200ml (7fl oz) skimmed milk
4 Canderel vanilla sticks
2 teaspoons vanilla flavouring
1 teaspoon ground cinnamon

- Blend the oat bran until fine and then combine with the rest of the bread ingredients in a small bowl. Stir together thoroughly. Pour this mixture into a rectangular microwavable container and microwave at 750W for 4 minutes. Turn the bread out of the container and leave to cool. Cut into nice thick slices.

- Make the eggy dip by breaking the eggs into a soup bowl and adding the milk, vanilla sticks, vanilla flavouring and cinnamon and whisking everything together with a fork.

- Heat a frying pan over a high heat and grease with a few drops of oil, wiping them off with kitchen paper. Dip the bread slices into the eggy mixture and cook each slice for 1–2 minutes on each side over a medium heat. Leave to cool slightly before serving.

Rhubarb Compote

4 servings | **Preparation time: 5 minutes**
Cooking time: 20 minutes

PV

500g (1lb 2oz) rhubarb, washed and trimmed
150ml (5fl oz) water
2 teaspoons vanilla flavouring
4 teaspoons crystallized stevia

- Chop the rhubarb into 1–2cm (½–¾in) pieces. (You could also use frozen rhubarb.)
- Place the rhubarb in a saucepan with the water and vanilla flavouring and cook over a low heat for about 20 minutes, stirring regularly. Check at regular intervals to make sure there is enough water in the pan and add a little more if necessary.
- Once the rhubarb is cooked, drain off any excess liquid and add the sweetener. Taste the compote to check that it is sweet enough and not too acidic.
- To ring the changes, you could also add some strawberry flavouring and/or rum flavouring.

Rhubarb Bavarois

4 servings | **Preparation time: 15 minutes**
Refrigeration time: overnight

PV

500g (1lb 2oz) rhubarb, washed and trimmed
150ml (5fl oz) water plus 3 tablespoons
6 Canderel vanilla sticks
6 gelatine leaves
Juice of ½ lemon
200g (7oz) fat-free fromage frais
1 teaspoon vanilla flavouring

- Chop the rhubarb into small chunks. (Alternatively, use frozen rhubarb.)

- Cook the rhubarb in a saucepan with 150ml (5fl oz) water for about 20 minutes. Once it is cooked, drain off any excess liquid and add the vanilla sticks. Taste and check that the stewed rhubarb is sweet enough and not too acidic, then blend it until the compote is a smooth purée.

- Soften the gelatine leaves in a bowl of cold water for 5 minutes, then drain and wring out. In a pan, heat the lemon juice with 3 tablespoons water. Add the gelatine leaves and dissolve them in the lemon water.

- Pour the gelatine mixture into the rhubarb purée. Add the fromage frais and vanilla flavouring. Check that the mixture is sweet enough, then pour into ramekin dishes or a bavarois mould and refrigerate overnight.

Rhubarb Tarte Tatin

4 servings | Preparation time: 20 minutes
Cooking time: 35 minutes

PV

500g (1lb 2oz) rhubarb, washed and trimmed
5 tablespoons Splenda granules
8 tablespoons oat bran
4 tablespoons wheat bran
8 tablespoons powdered skimmed milk
4 eggs
8 tablespoons fat-free fromage frais
2 teaspoons liquid Hermesetas

- Preheat the oven to 180°C/350°F/Gas 4.

- Chop the rhubarb into small chunks (or use frozen rhubarb, defrosted). Sprinkle some of the sweetener over the bottom of a glass or silicone pie dish and carefully arrange the rhubarb chunks on top. Sprinkle over some more sweetener and bake in the preheated oven for 5–10 minutes to caramelize the rhubarb, but be careful not to let it burn.

- Meanwhile, in a bowl, mix together the oat and wheat brans with the powdered skimmed milk. Stir in the eggs and beat the mixture vigorously so that it becomes nice and frothy. Add the fromage frais and liquid sweetener.

- Check that the rhubarb in the oven is nicely caramelized and taste a chunk to see whether it is sweet enough. If necessary add more sweetener.

- Pour the bran mixture over the caramelized rhubarb and bake in the preheated oven for 15 minutes. Then lower the temperature to 160°C/325°F/Gas 3 and bake for a further 10 minutes, sprinkling a little more sweetener over the top. Turn the tarte tatin out on to a serving dish, with the rhubarb on top. It is delicious served either hot or slightly warm.

Rhubarb and Strawberry Meringue Pie

4 servings | **Preparation time: 20 minutes**
Cooking time: 48 minutes

PV

---

5 eggs
150g (5½oz) fat-free natural yoghurt
4 tablespoons oat bran
2 tablespoons wheat bran
3 teaspoons liquid Hermesetas
600g (1lb 5oz) rhubarb, washed and trimmed
2 teaspoons strawberry flavouring
Pinch of salt
1 teaspoon vanilla flavouring

- Preheat the oven to 180°C/350°F/Gas 4.

- Break 2 of the eggs into a bowl and whisk them together with the yoghurt, then add the oat and wheat brans and ½ teaspoon of the liquid sweetener. Pour into a pie dish lined with greaseproof paper (or a silicone dish) and blind-bake in the preheated oven for 15 minutes, keeping a careful eye on the pastry case so that it does not overcook.

- Chop the rhubarb into small chunks (or use frozen rhubarb, defrosted). Break the 3 remaining eggs into a bowl, but retain 2 egg whites to use later on. Whisk the eggs with 2 teaspoons of the liquid sweetener and the strawberry flavouring. Remove the pie base from the oven, arrange the rhubarb on top and pour over the beaten eggs. Bake in the oven for 25 minutes.

- In the meantime, beat the 2 reserved egg whites with the salt until very stiff. Add the remaining ½ teaspoon liquid sweetener and the vanilla flavouring. Continue whisking for a few minutes. When the pie is ready, remove from the oven and use a piping bag to decorate the top with the meringue. Return the pie to the oven for a further 7–8 minutes until the meringue is golden brown – take care that it does not burn.

Rhubarb Topped with Panna Cotta

4 servings | **Preparation time: 10 minutes** | **Cooking time: 25 minutes**
Refrigeration time: overnight

PV

500g (1lb 2oz) rhubarb, washed and trimmed
150ml (5fl oz) water
4 teaspoons vanilla flavouring
6 teaspoons crystallized stevia
900g (2lb) thick fat-free natural yoghurt
100ml (3½fl oz) skimmed milk
2 × 2g sachets agar-agar

■ Chop the rhubarb into 1–2cm (½–¾in) pieces. (You could also use frozen rhubarb.) Place the rhubarb chunks in a saucepan with the water and 1 teaspoon of the vanilla flavouring and cook over a low heat for about 20 minutes, stirring regularly. Keep checking to make sure there is enough water in the pan and add a little more if you need to. Once the rhubarb is cooked, drain off any excess liquid and add 4 teaspoons of the sweetener. Taste the compote to check that it is sweet enough and not too acidic.

■ In a bowl, mix the yoghurt very thoroughly with the remaining 2 teaspoons sweetener and 3 teaspoons vanilla flavouring. Heat the skimmed milk in a small saucepan over a low heat and add the agar-agar, stirring well. Bring to the boil and remove the pan from the heat, stirring all the while. Add the milk to the yoghurt and mix everything together.

■ Pour the rhubarb compote into the bottom of four glass sundae dishes and cover with the panna cotta mixture. Leave to cool to room temperature, then refrigerate overnight.

Rhubarb Clafoutis

4 servings | **Preparation time: 10 minutes**
Cooking time: 35 minutes

PV

600g (1lb 5oz) rhubarb, washed and trimmed
8 tablespoons Splenda granules
4 eggs
2 tablespoons cornflour
400ml (14fl oz) skimmed milk
2 tablespoons vanilla flavouring

■ Preheat the oven to 180°C/350°F/Gas 4.

■ Chop the rhubarb into 2cm (¾in) pieces (or use
frozen rhubarb, defrosted) and arrange in an
ovenproof dish. Sprinkle over 2 tablespoons of the
sweetener and bake in the preheated oven for about
10 minutes, to soften the rhubarb.

■ Meanwhile, mix the eggs in a bowl with 5 tablespoons
of the sweetener. Dissolve the cornflour in a little
of the milk and add to the sweetened eggs. Pour
in the rest of the skimmed milk and add the vanilla
flavouring.

■ Pour this mixture over the rhubarb and sprinkle the
remaining tablespoon of sweetener on top. Bake in
the oven for 25 minutes, keeping a careful eye on the
clafoutis to check when it is ready. It is delicious eaten
either warm or cold.

Pink Rhubarb, Verbena and Mint Soup

4 servings | **Preparation time: 20 minutes** | **Cooking time: 20 minutes**
Refrigeration time: 30 minutes

PV

600g (1lb 5oz) rhubarb, washed and trimmed
400ml (14fl oz) water
1 tablespoon vanilla flavouring
6 teaspoons crystallized stevia
6 sprigs fresh verbena
8 mint leaves

- Partly peel the stalks to remove some of the stringy bits and chop the rhubarb into 5cm (2in) pieces.

- Put the rhubarb in a saucepan with the water and add the vanilla flavouring. Bring to the boil and cook over a gentle heat for about 20 minutes. When the rhubarb is ready the water will have turned pink. Add the sweetener and remove the pan from the heat.

- Wash and dry the sprigs of verbena. Pick the leaves off 3 of the sprigs, chop, and add to the soup. Finely chop 4 of the mint leaves and add to the soup.

- Leave to cool and then refrigerate for 30 minutes. Taste to see if the soup is sweet enough and add more sweetener if necessary. Divide between four bowls and decorate with the remaining verbena leaves and mint leaves. Serve well chilled.

Mango Lassi

4 servings | **Preparation time: 10 minutes**
Refrigeration time: 30 minutes minimum

PP - PV

600g (1lb 5oz) thick fat-free natural yoghurt
300ml (10fl oz) skimmed milk
4 teaspoons crystallized stevia
1 teaspoon mango flavouring

- Put all the ingredients in a blender, stir and then blend for 2 minutes.
- Pour the lassi mixture into four large glasses and refrigerate for at least 30 minutes. Serve well chilled.
- You can create many different lassis by using a variety of flavourings: fruit-flavoured lassis, such as this mango version; salty lassis; lassis with rose water and so on.

Coffee Milkshake

4 servings | **Preparation time: 10 minutes**
Refrigeration time: 1 hour

PP - PV

120g (4¼oz) fat-free fromage frais
120g (4¼oz) virtually fat-free quark
500ml (18fl oz) skimmed milk
4 teaspoons instant coffee granules
4 teaspoons crystallized stevia
1 tablespoon vanilla flavouring
4 coffee beans, to decorate

- Place the fromage frais and quark in the freezer for 1 hour.

- Remove the fromage frais and quark from the freezer. Place the skimmed milk, coffee, sweetener and vanilla flavouring in a blender. Add the fromage frais and quark and blend everything for 2 minutes.

- Serve the milkshakes in four glasses with a straw and a coffee bean for decoration. If you wish, you could finish off with some Dukan Chantilly (see page 152).

Mango and Lychees in Rose Water Jelly

4 servings | **Preparation time: 15 minutes** | **Cooking time: 5 minutes**
Refrigeration time: 1 hour minimum

C

---

1 large mango, ripe but still firm
20 lychees
4 gelatine leaves
200ml (7fl oz) water
6 tablespoons rose water
6 tablespoons Canderel granules
Mint leaves, to decorate

- Peel the mango and cut into 2cm (¾in) cubes. Place in a bowl in the fridge. Peel the lychees, remove the stones and place in another bowl in the fridge.
- Soak the gelatine leaves in a bowl of cold water for 5 minutes to soften them, and then drain. Put the gelatine in a small saucepan with 50ml (2fl oz) of the water and leave to dissolve over a very low heat, stirring at regular intervals.
- Take the pan off the heat and add the remaining 150ml (5fl oz) water along with the rose water, stirring gently. Add the sweetener.
- Put the pan in the fridge for about 30 minutes until the jelly starts to set, then take it out.
- Drain the fruit and divide among four wide sundae dishes, pouring in a little jelly between each layer of fruit. Place in the fridge to set completely.
- Keep in the fridge until ready to serve, and then decorate with the mint leaves.

Summer Fruit Conserve with Agar-agar

4 servings | **Preparation time: 15 minutes**
Cooking time: 10 minutes

C

500g (1lb 2oz) assorted red summer fruits (except cherries)
8 tablespoons Splenda granules
200ml (7fl oz) water
2 × 2g sachets agar-agar
800ml (28fl oz) apple juice
2 teaspoons morello cherry flavouring

- Cook the fruit in a saucepan with the sweetener and water for 5–6 minutes.

- In another pan, dissolve the agar-agar in the apple juice. Add the fruit and stir, then add the morello cherry flavouring. Bring to the boil and cook for a further 3–4 minutes, stirring the fruit very gently.

- Pour the conserve into glass yoghurt pots with a lid or other small glass jars and seal straightaway. Always use glass containers that have been sterilized beforehand.

- You can use this conserve to add a fruity touch to your yoghurts, dairy products and galettes. It will keep in the fridge for a week.

Spiced Pear Ring

**4 servings | Preparation time: 10 minutes | Cooking time: 20 minutes
Refrigeration time: 4 hours minimum**

C

---

6 gelatine leaves
4 pears, peeled, cored and halved
1 cinnamon stick
1 clove
2 star anis
Grated zest of 1 unwaxed orange
250ml (9fl oz) water
1 teaspoon cognac flavouring
8 Canderel vanilla sticks

- Soak the gelatine leaves in a bowl of cold water for 5 minutes to soften them.

- Place the pears in a saucepan along with the spices and orange zest. Add the water and cognac flavouring and cook, covered, over a low heat for 20 minutes.

- Take the pan off the heat and leave to cool for a few minutes. Use a slotted spoon to remove the pears and spices from the liquid. Drain the softened gelatine leaves, add to the liquid in the pan along with the vanilla sticks and stir well.

- Arrange the pears around the sides of a ring-shaped mould, preferably silicone, and pour in the liquid from the pan. Refrigerate for at least 4 hours until set.

Blueberry and Violet Muffins

4 servings | **Preparation time: 10 minutes**
Cooking time: 30 minutes

C

---

4 tablespoons fat-free natural yoghurt
4 eggs
4 tablespoons Splenda granules
2 teaspoons violet flavouring
8 tablespoons oat bran
4 tablespoons wheat bran
1 teaspoon baking powder
150g (5½oz) blueberries (fresh or frozen)

- Preheat the oven to 180°C/350°F/Gas 4.

- In a bowl, combine the yoghurt, eggs, sweetener and violet flavouring. Add the oat and wheat brans and the baking powder and continue stirring. Add the blueberries and mix them in carefully.

- Pour the mixture into silicone muffin moulds and bake in the preheated oven for about 30 minutes, keeping a careful eye on the muffins. They are cooked once they turn golden brown on top.

Minty Red Fruit Smoothie

4 servings | Preparation time: 5 minutes

C

600g (1lb 5oz) thick fat-free natural yoghurt
300g (10½ oz) mixed frozen red fruit (strawberries, raspberries,
blackcurrants, blueberries, etc.), defrosted
8 mint leaves (or 1 teaspoon peppermint flavouring)
4 teaspoons crystallized stevia
4 tablespoons oat bran
250ml (9fl oz) skimmed milk
6 ice cubes

- Put all the ingredients into a blender. Blend for at least 1½ minutes so that the mixture is really smooth.
- Pour the smoothie mixture into four large glasses and serve immediately.

Iced Apple Meringue

4 servings | Preparation time: 10 minutes
Cooking time: 10 minutes | Refrigeration time: 5 hours minimum

C

---

4 apples, peeled and cored
Grated zest and juice of 1 unwaxed lemon
1 teaspoon ground cinnamon
3 egg whites
Pinch of salt
4 Canderel vanilla sticks

- Cut the apples into pieces and pour over the lemon juice to stop them from discolouring.
- Put the apple pieces in a microwavable dish, sprinkle over the cinnamon, cover the dish with a lid and microwave for about 6 minutes (alternatively, steam for about 10 minutes).
- The apples should be soft enough to purée easily. Leave the purée to cool.
- Stir the lemon zest into the apple purée. Beat the egg whites with the salt until stiff. Gently fold the beaten egg whites into the apple purée and add the vanilla sticks.
- Pour the mixture into four large dishes and refrigerate for at least 5 hours.